OPEN THE BLEED OFF

UNLEASHING MENTAL HEALTH
IN THE WORKPLACE

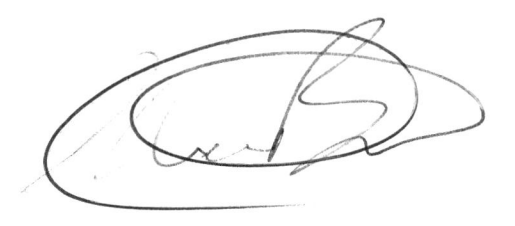

STEVE BEEDIE

For my father

ACKNOWLEDGMENTS

I want to express my profound gratitude to an incredible group of people who have supported me in bringing this book to life. Writing a book is a monumental task, especially for someone who hails from a humble background in Banff.

Firstly, immense respect goes out to my friends who dedicated their time to read parts of the manuscript and offered invaluable feedback. A special shoutout to Simon Maryan, who not only provided guidance on challenging sections but also shared many laughs over sausage butties and wine. Your support has been a cornerstone in this journey.

To my mates who constantly encouraged me during the years I procrastinated on this book.

A deep admiration and respect to every single person I've ever worked with during my fifteen years working around the world in oil and gas. Not enough time and respect is given to you, the sacrifices and effort you put in each trip away from those you love. From the people who sail the ships, to the crews who drill the well, to the engineers who worked alongside us, to the hundreds and thousands of you who work under stress in the offices on the beach, i have a special message within the book for you. But for now, you have my respect.

Suds, your unwavering support has always made my dreams feel valid, even when others doubted them. Your genuine friendship means the world to me. Tosh, your humour, and kind-heartedness have been a beacon of hope, always lifting me up during tough times. Darren, your intelligent and compassionate feedback has been a source of constant motivation. Chelle, your persistent inquiries about the book's progress and your straightforward encouragement have been so helpful. Ellie, my niece, your kind words and messages have always been a source of joy – and I promise to take better care of your car in the future!

To my brother, Mark, your honesty and straightforward advice have kept me grounded and focused, especially through tough times. Your unwavering support means more than words can express. Lynnie, my sister-in-law, your strength and kindness have been a source of inspiration. Your support has been a guiding light.

Jack, my son, watching you grow up has been an incredible journey. Your transition into adulthood fills me with immense pride and love.

I am also deeply grateful to all the companies and individuals who have been part of my speaking career. Your belief in my work has been a true blessing. To my offshore colleagues, your camaraderie and spirit have left an indelible mark on my heart.

A heartfelt thank you to my friends who shared their stories for this book. Your contributions have enriched this project beyond measure. Caitlin, your words have touched many lives, and I am grateful for your involvement.

And finally, to you, the reader, I hope these pages offer you a glimmer of hope and resonate with you, even if just for a moment.

Thank you all for being part of this incredible journey.

TABLE OF CONTENTS

ACKNOWLEDGMENTS iii
INTRODUCTION xvii
    A World That Isn't Open xxvi
    Stress xxxiv
PART ONE: A WORKPLACE LACKING PURPOSE 1
    High Pressure Blowout Low Pressure Leak 14
    The Hidden Costs Of A Closed World 24
    Stretching Away From Shame 30
PART TWO: A NEW APPROACH TO MENTAL HEALTH IN THE WORKPLACE 40
    Making The Connection 53
    Embracing Open Heartedness In A World Of Challenges 58
    Mental Health In Energy 62
    Making The Connection 65
    The Unspoken Method 78
PART HREE: LEADING TO PROMOTE MENTAL HEALTH 95
    Help– The Second Step In The Unspoken Method 98
    Help - The Power Of Unspoken Kindness 98
PART FOUR: MOBILISING A MENTALLY FIT WORKFORCE: EMBRACING HELP, IMPLEMENTING THE UNSPOKEN METHOD 104
    Hope - Illuminating The Path Ahead In The Unspoken Method 108

Embracing Help: The Power Of A Stronger Leader 115

PART FIVE: NAVIGATING WORKPLACE MENTAL HEALTH CHALLENGES 118

Heal – The Final Step In The Unspoken Method 122

PART SIX: DISCOVERING PURPOSE FOR WORKPLACE MENTAL HEALTH 136

The Power Of Openness: Embracing The Wisdom In The Wound ... 140

Choices And Chances 143

CONCLUSION 150

STANDING TALL: A Tribute to the Heroes of the Oil and Gas Industry 152

BONUS CHAPTER: THE BEAUTY OF PAIN: UNVEILING THE MOST FUNDAMENTAL REALITY 157

FINAL THOUGHTS 160

I have known Steve for several years. He has been of great help to me and my trauma team in its work. He seems inexhaustible in his own efforts to help people. I am also impressed by how imaginative he is; he works very hard to ensure his plans come to fruition. On several occasions, he and I have made presentations together to, for example, undergraduate students. He tells of his own experiences sensitively and movingly. In particular, he is helpfully frank about how they have affected him and his family. What he is currently doing and seeks to do represents an essential contribution to the welfare of all who care to make a change.

– PROFESSOR DAVID A ALEXANDER MA(HONS), C. PSYCHOL, PHD, FBPS, FRSM, (HON)FRCPSYCH

"Steve recently shared his inspiring story with Kellas as part of an offsite team development day for our staff. He was brilliantly engaging and spoke openly and honestly about his journey from a challenging upbringing to his military career and subsequent mental health struggles. The focus of our team day was well-being in the workplace, and Steve's talk added a heartfelt and personal element to the agenda."

KELLAS MIDSTREAM

Dear Steve, Thanks again for your help the other day during filming. Thanks especially for speaking so frankly; I'm keeping your number to pester you again! (Keep the mobile off) Regards.

REEVEL ALDERSON,
HOME AFFAIRS CORRESPONDENT BBC.

Steve's experiences and story were an inspiring workshop in November 2009 with our 4th-year occupational therapy students. Steve's engaged the students and enabled them to appreciate the many challenges and health problems that war veterans can experience when they leave the military.

We look forward to Steve being part of our student's learning and development again.

> STEPHANIE MORRISON - LECTURER IN OCCUPATIONAL THERAPY, THE ROBERT GORDON UNIVERSITY

Steve, we have had really good feedback from the session, especially from the workshops (which are generally a tough crowd)

Thank you so much and thank you for your time today and for speaking from the heart; your enthusiasm for all things mental health is apparent, and you are making a fantastic difference in people's lives.

> ACE WINCHES

Outline: What this book will give you

Introduction: Open the Bleed Off - A world that isn't open

PART 1: A WORKPLACE LACKING PURPOSE

The Assumption of Understanding

Ineffective Workplace Motivation Tactics

PART 2: A NEW APPROACH TO MENTAL HEALTH IN THE WORKPLACE

The Golden Triangle of Workplace Well-being

The Biological Connection Between Purpose and Mental Health at Work

Cultivating Clarity, Discipline, and Consistency in the Workplace

PART 3: LEADING WITH PURPOSE TO PROMOTE MENTAL HEALTH

Establishing Trust in Leadership

Creating a Tipping Point for Workplace Mental Health

PART 4: MOBILISING A MENTALLY FIT WORKFORCE

Embrace the WHY, Implement the HOW

Aligning Purpose and Action in the Workplace

The Art of Active Listening and Effective Communication

PART 5: OVERCOMING WORKPLACE MENTAL HEALTH CHALLENGES

Navigating the Complexities of Success

Managing Organisational Disconnects

PART 6: DISCOVERING PURPOSE FOR WORKPLACE MENTAL HEALTH

The Roots of Purpose-Driven Mental Health

Embracing New Frontiers of Competition and Collaboration

Conclusion: The Future of Mental Health in the Workplace

Acknowledgements Notes

What this book will give you!

It will open a clear path to understanding how simple conversations about mental health can have the most incredible impact on your teams, staff, business, and even your family.

You can approach it in a much lighter way when you see how important it is to talk about this subject without worrying about how serious or complex it can be, just as safety was a massive just speaking about it all those years ago. The macho culture and masculinity around safety kept us from the shift. It took a hugely impactful event for us to look at safety in our industry more profoundly—a human way.

This new way is what we are approaching now. We are losing people. Your friends who you work with. Family members and colleagues from around the industry aren't just taking their own lives by suicide; they are now doing it at work. It's become the silent scream none of us can ignore. It may only seem like a few people, but one is too many in my world. Sadly, you will know that the numbers are growing each year.

Many of us are trying hard to speak about this genuinely and openly. I want to tear the plaster off and start opening up with heart, passion, and an open mind. I know it's just a book. I realise it will not become a best seller. But we can make a difference if I can reach many people emotionally with your help.

How can this book help you?

This book will help you open those areas of emotion you find hard to talk about. It will help you navigate these conversations when others are trying to be open with you and you're feeling a little closed off. It will help you, those around you, and others you had no idea were holding back from asking for help with their struggles. This book will help. And if we only reach a handful of people, at least it's a handful of support that our industry needs.

The One Belief: Speaking Is Healing.

In a world filled with uncertainty, we want to seek novel solutions. The human psyche is hardwired to recognise that new experiences can either a signal of danger or hold the promise of remarkable rewards. Your journey through "Open the Bleed Off" is a unique opportunity.

Speaking about your feelings is a healing act. Surrounded by judgement all these years has hardened you and many people around your life to choose a colder way of life. Not having caring conversations holds you back from the deeper connection you can have with those you care about. Yeah, it's scary at first but as you take a wander across this book you will uncover conversations with real people and their stories will inspire you to seek a simpler attitude that can open your life and business up to knowing the truth of relationships. Speaking is healing. And healing is something we need right now.

This fresh perspective beckons to the innate explorer within you. So, take hold of this belief and have a moment of courage, an open mind and the desire to help just one person, even if that person is yourself. Together, we can reduce uncertainty, lower stress, and embrace the power of seeing the world from a new perspective.

What is the ONE thing you truly want from a book about mental health and well-being? Is it the knowledge to create a more compassionate workplace, the ability to engage in meaningful conversations, or the power to change lives, including your own? 'Open the Bleed Off' is vital to fulfilling this fundamental desire. I cannot do the work for you. I can only offer a new way of seeing the impact a few conversations can have on people, but this is the start of something new. A desire to change is all it takes for things to shift.

As you embark on this journey, you'll discover that 'Open the Bleed Off' is not just another book—it's the ONLY way forward. The New Method will guide you to open up the conversations that matter to you, foster understanding with your friends and colleagues you care about, and transform these relationships to hold a truer essence that feels richer and of much more quality.

This book is your indispensable tool for navigating the uncharted waters of mental health conversations with grace, empathy, and genuine impact.

This idea stands apart because it doesn't focus on supplying facts and statistics about mental health to give you information; it opens the door to authentic, transformative conversations. The UK is heavily weighed down by the rising costs of lost time from people we know who are desperate for rest or time off. That number is sitting at £100 Billion plus (last time I checked, it was £110 Billion and climbing, which is 4.5% of GDP). If we look at the facts alone, we miss the opportunity to see the people. And this is a mistake that has caused us to walk down this path in the first place. Seeing people as statistics is a zero-sum game. We need to look at this problem with a new lens. A more open lens where more significant portions of light can come in. It's time to open up.

Unlike other resources that may scratch the surface, this book delves deep into the heart of the matter, offering real-world stories, practical guidance that anyone can use, and a fresh perspective that makes discussing mental health not only easy but crucial.

Imagine gaining the power to change your workplace culture, strengthen your relationships, and enhance your well-being. 'Open the Bleed Off' promises you the key to unlock these profound transformations. By reading this book, you'll learn how to open conversations that matter, creating a ripple effect that will positively change your life, teams, and business. It's not just a book; it's a simple and fresh way of connecting with the people around you.

The authenticity of 'Open the Bleed Off' lies in my journey. From a struggling young father, battling PTSD, depression and anxiety after a horrible medical discharge from my devoted military career, which pushed me into a dark identity crisis followed by a brutal marriage breakdown and a series of hardships, including homelessness, alcohol abuse, fighting, and a reluctance to admit I was breaking. I realised that I had to make a change. I needed help. Asking for this help took all my courage as I had been through a tumultuous battle coming out of the army, and no one was available to help me. There were no mental health influencers or teams to speak to, and no aid was nearby. I had to figure this out all on my own. I turned this mammoth task on its head through conversations shared online and in person and eventually began to help others. I became the solution I never had. Now, I reach millions online and in person yearly through my talks, events and podcasts; my story proves the power of open conversations. I've shared real stories, natural solutions, and actual results.

The actual obstacle is the culture of silence that surrounds mental health. We've been conditioned to believe that vulnerability is a sign of weakness, and this belief holds us back from engaging in the conversations we desperately need. 'Open the Bleed Off' reveals this invisible barrier and shows you how to shatter it, opening the door to healing and growth. And this is needed now more than ever. Waiting for someone else to help will never be the solution. I have embraced that a single person has enough passion and power to make even a tiny dent in this universal problem, and with a bit of help, we can reach even more.

The enemy we face together is the age-old belief that speaking about mental health is taboo, that it's not 'manly' to share your struggles, and that it's best to keep quiet about your pain. 'Open the Bleed Off' confronts this outdated thinking and shares a new perspective that empowers you to break free from its grip. Women and men face this enemy together; we are all in this battle. Mental health doesn't care what colour, creed, or sex you are. It just uses you where you are.

The need for open conversations undiluted by stigma has never been more urgent in today's world. People are silently suffering, and it's affecting our workplaces, our families, and our communities. The book addresses this pressing issue and provides a timely solution that will help you navigate the challenges of our times. I know you are feeling it. We all are. You have a chance right here and now in this book to begin finally seeing there is a way across this dark void we face. I know you are struggling with some pressure and that if only there were a way to release some of this pressure, you could help yourself and, with a bit of trust, a few others, too. Helping people matters.

Is trust earned? I've gained some through years of dedication to mental health advocacy. I've spoken on stages across industries, coached those in need, and shared my heart with the world. My passion and results speak for themselves. But I have yet to start to be what I desire. I want to embrace more than a few talks and speaking engagements; I want to inspire you, which is why I've written this book for you. So you can tap into that uniqueness inside you and find a way to help you open the bleed-off when you are struggling. Please feel inspired to pass on the message within this book. We all need to ask for help. There is a strength in needing people; we all must be okay with asking for more help.

The book works by guiding you through the art of open conversations about mental health. It supplies practical techniques, real-life examples, and step-by-step instructions to help you start these conversations, fostering understanding, empathy, and lasting change. And I realise it will feel a little funny, trying to be the person who brings a new idea to a conversation, especially at work, but let's be honest. We need it. It would help if you had it. Our industry dam well needs it. I believe in this idea so much I have left full-time work from having dealt with too much pressure and stress to be the man I should have been a few years ago. I recently lost my father (August 2023). I was devastated; I still find it hard to talk or think about it, but I am here, working and creating something of value to be a small beacon of hope in an otherwise bleak world that is so toxic and wrapped in ego. I hope we can find a gentler way together.

It's never easy changing how you see yourself and others in the world. It's going to take a little courage on your part. I have a feeling that you care about this, this wonderful moment of humanity where we are navigating the treacherous waters of wellness. Some think we need to be stoic and strong; others believe we need to batten down the emotional hatches and stay focused on growing through it. Some feel it's a waste of time and energy and this is alla bunch of bullshit. I believe it's the greatest conversation we've ever had or will have and if we open up about this with a sense of adventure and hope we can invite a new presence and attitude to being there for people and those who are struggling. This experience is available to you, right now all you need is to open up a little about the struggles you've had, listen to others sharing their tiredness and stress. And let the moment take shape as it needs to. You don't need to push and pull at it. Allow the shape of the conversation to be natural. Like an uncovering. The flower only needs to be touched by light for it to open in the morning. No motivation or nudging. It just is. So as you turn the page remember to notice the feelings you have. Don't force them or deny them. Allow the moment to flow through you. And let it open up as the warmth touches you.

Getting started is as simple as picking up this book and diving into the first chapter. The insights and tools inside offer immediate help and guidance. They will set you on a transformative journey towards healthier, more open relationships.

By embracing 'Open the Bleed Off,' you have nothing to lose and everything to gain. You stand to gain a deeper understanding of mental health, stronger relationships, a more compassionate workplace, and personal well-being. The only thing to lose is the silence that has held you back for far too long.

INTRODUCTION

"Son, get yourself offshore. That's where the money is," my father voice was strong and calm, like his mood. He always kept a sense of himself that people respected deeply. He advised from his seat which you could almost always find him in if he wasn't outside doing some DIY or building another outhouse or fixing the roof. One time, after his lung transplant the doctor came to visit him and after no answer to the doorbell, the doc was concerned and opened the door gingerly asking for my dad.

"Bryon, Bryon are you there?". Nothing.

The doc pushed the heavy brown door open and again asked after my dad but there was no answer, so he walked further into the house and then he noticed a plastic line coming from the kitchen leading outside into the back garden. It was the clear airline that was on my dad's tank. He panicked and rushed outside following the line like the red and yellow stripes you sometimes see in the hospital emergency wards. As the doctor stepped into the garden and the sunshine smacked his face, he had to look up in utter disbelief. My father was perched on the roof of the house fixing the lead that had been damaged in the storms, the airline was there with him, along with the tank of oxygen that was meant to be sitting next to his chair. One thing about my father, he never let the old man in. So when my dad told me to get myself offshore. I knew i had to listen.

Having recently left the army after serving in two wars, four tours of duty and losing a lot of mates to suicide i was struggling with PTSD from seeing kids murdered, people blown up or shot, villages burned to the ground and cities levelled. depression and a tonne of stress was pushing my body to the brink and my mind to the edge. I was not myself and felt lost, and now a father myself and trying to navigate a world that felt alien to me, I felt a directionless drift taking over my life. I envisioned a fulfilling career that would make my father proud and stabilise my son's life and give us a better future. I looked up to my father, his seasoned wisdom a beacon in my unsettled world.

"Dad, how do I get offshore? I need to build a stable career, not just jump from one small job to another and I'm honestly not enjoying these stupid little jobs." I earnestly desired to reclaim the sense of purpose the army had once given me.

He offered a reassuring smile, a gesture that symbolised hope and the potential for something better. Yet, reality bore me an enormous mountain of hurdles: financial instability, lack of resources, and a life paralysed by the unseen scars from the battlefield. The idea of venturing into a new career felt like a colossal task from the deep hole I found myself in, especially with the PTSD that clung to me like the frost of winters first day, a silent yet overwhelming cold presence.

In 2007, mental health was barely a whisper in the circles I frequented, a taboo subject too often brushed under the rug. It seemed like men had conditioned themselves to keep it all bottled up, allowing pressure to build to a breaking point until an inevitable explosion occurred. I experienced this first hand: a volatile combination of suppressed emotions and traumatic memories led to a significant altercation with the police. This rock bottom signalled a desperate need for change.

Haunted by horrific scenes from Kosovo and Iraq, seeing children blown apart or gunned down, and watching entire towns burned to a cinder for the faith they believed in. I was a troubled, unwell young man carrying the unbearable weight of loss and guilt; I felt lost in a world devoid of compassion and understanding. I watched fellow service members succumb to the dark claws of depression. I, too, danced dangerously close to that edge, driven by an agonising secret etched into my soul from my time in the war.

Christmas Eve, a time meant for joy and fun, reminded me of my desperate situation: jobless, skint, and facing eviction. Yet, amidst the darkness, a laugh bubbled up, perhaps a sound steeped in madness but carrying a flicker of hope and a budding idea spark.

"I must find a way through this," I found myself whispering, a promise to my son and a pledge to myself to forge a path to a future worth living.

Men don't talk about this stuff. We hold it all in, pressing down on the trauma, the fear, and the unspoken realities that are too raw to touch. It was as if speaking it would make it real, a confession of weakness in a world that demanded an iron spine. Even women, whom society expects to be the caregivers, the nurturers, were swallowed by the same oppressive silence, their experiences dismissed, their voices stifled in a systemic cycle of disregard.

As I sat there, staring at the eviction notice in hand, laughter bubbled up inside me, breaking through the dread. Laughter, a fractured sound that held no joy, yet within it, a spark of rebellion ignited, a desperate refusal to be hushed. It was an acknowledgement of the absurdity, the tragedy, and the unbearable weight of expectations that life had thrown my way.

Men and women alike, we were all trapped in a dance of pretences, affixing masks of invulnerability even as the ground beneath us trembled and threatened to swallow us whole.

Fifteen years have passed since that desperate laugh echoed in my bleak surroundings. To say I have "found a way" would be an understatement. I survived, persevered, and eventually thrived, even when life threw its worst at me: cancer, PTSD, depression, homelessness, loss of loved ones, and heart-wrenching betrayals. As i write this i am trying to hold back from opening, that's how powerful this stuff is. Me the author trying to hold back. I guess this stuff runs deeper than we like to admit. I feel it just like you, the resistance to stay normal, to keep within the safety of common ground and never venture out. Yet something has always stirred inside of me. A rebellious streak of darkness and hope that is transfixed on making things better. Tastier than it is or has been. As i reach these first few words i think it's only fair that i open about some unspoken things. How else can i expect you to do the same.

I come from a broken home. My biological father walked out of my existence when I was only three months old. I searched for answers even as a young boy as I fought with the notion that I am, in fact, a mistake, an unwanted thing, easily cast aside and ignored. The crazy part is he wasn't far away, only a single mile away my entire childhood. So, either my biological parents held some unspoken secret about how I was a mistake, or the truth is, I was simply not worthy enough of his love. It was the 80s, and things were slightly more secretive around children without dads. I know for me, anyway, it was a territory that was never really talked about much, and whenever I did, it was not welcomed. I guess my mum felt ashamed or abandoned, and I understood this deeply. I remember the days in school when all the kids had to write Father's Day cards, and I would be the only kid in class sitting in silence, doing nothing but pretending everyone couldn't see me.

A fatherless boy and I felt unwanted. Their silence was deafening to me. It was so defeating, apart from the rage it caused me to learn early on, and it came out in all the ways you can imagine. I ran away from home a lot, taking solace in the woods, often staying hidden for days, causing my mum to lose her shit and go mad with worry wondering all sorts of upsetting things as I was playing my game of "fuck the world" as my anger turned into smarts. I would learn to navigate the world without much money or access to things like other kids. All my clothes were hand-me-downs and jumble sale smelly crap. My only saving grace was my grandfather. He was a man's man: a good, soft-hearted, kind soul who always loved me being around his feet. I would spend countless days by his side helping tend to his tatties in the back garden and enjoy his sun-kissed arm sweating away as he looked so strong. His smile was a beaming ray of light.

I stand here today as a testament to resilience, acknowledging the struggles, triumphs, and small victories won through the hard lessons learned. I found happiness amidst the chaos and a deeper understanding of the intricacies of the human condition. I embraced the flaws and imperfections that make us beautifully human, striving to help others find their paths through shared experiences and open hearts.

Yet, even with the wisdom gathered over the years, I faced the cold and uncaring demands of the corporate world, a stark reminder that society still often prioritises profit over empathy and understanding. A realisation dawned upon me as I navigated grief and the pressure of unsustainable expectations: I had no control over others, only how I chose to respond.

Men are raised tough and rigid and expected to be like mountains, unyielding and stoic, but even mountains erode; even mountains break under the correct pressure. It was a toxic loop, where admitting you were hurting was seen as a fault line, a dangerous crack in a meticulously constructed facade. It was a workplace where compassion had no place, where human needs and aches were considered liabilities rather than truths to be acknowledged and respected. Women suppressed their nurturing instincts, petrified of being perceived as overly emotional or incapable. At the same time, men harboured the notion that to be strong, one had to be unbreakable, devoid of fears and tears. But we were not rocks; we were flesh and bone, heart and soul, bled and broke.

I found myself yet again at the mercy of the oppressive demands of a toxic work environment, where personal struggles are pushed to the side and expected to take a back seat to the unyielding demands of the job. It was a world where men and women quietly erected walls around themselves, trapping their true feelings and fears within a fortress of enforced stoicism. I refused to be silent, a rejection of the unhealthy maxims that dictated our lives.

As I stood alone at my desk, a day after burying my father, I found the courage to speak my truth, to expose the raw and aching wound to the light. To admit that I was not okay, that the pressure was too much, a crushing weight on my already burdened shoulders. Yet, the response was as cold as it was predictable, dismissing my pain in favour of the relentless march toward profit and efficiency.

I'd had enough. I was tired of trying to fit into a mould with no space for humanity, for the deep and intricate tapestry of emotions that make us who we are. Nurturing women were forced into shells of hardness, and the men transformed into silent soldiers on a battlefield devoid of empathy; we were all victims of a culture that prized results over people, a machine that ground the beauty and complexity of human emotions into dust. I'm not saying people are evil or have no feelings; I'm simply saying that the toxicity of work had ingrained our actions into a movement of profit over people and getting everything done for the client's good, not the other way around. People can only take so much. If you think otherwise, then this book is not for you.

With a heart carrying the weight of unspoken stories and a spirit eager to dismantle the toxic narratives that held us hostage, I chose to open the bleed-off. It was an act of survival, of reclaiming the space to breathe, to grieve, to be vulnerable and natural in a world that constantly demanded we be anything but ourselves. I wanted to be more who I was, to stop pretending I was a macho soldier or a man of iron. I can be those things while holding my gentle ideals close to my heart, and by being more myself, I could embrace a more straightforward, more compassionate way of living.

The road ahead was uncertain, but the path was clear. It was time to challenge the narratives that held me captive, to foster environments where people could show up as they were, scars, fears, and all. It was time to reject the toxic masculinity that stifled my voice. These damaging expectations snuffed out the nurturing spirit of women who dared to care and feel.

Through this book, I embark on a journey to unravel the tightly wound cord of societal expectations to expose the raw, pulsating truth of human experience. It invites both men and women to cast aside the stifling armour we never wished to wear. To embrace the full spectrum of our humanity with courage and compassion.

In a world where we are rebels in a war, we never signed up for, it is a call to lay down our arms, open the bleed-off, and find the courage to be vulnerable and beautifully human.

I chose to open, to share my turmoil and pain with a listening ear, venting the swirling whirlpool of anger, sadness, and frustration that threatened to engulf me. I prioritised my well-being over society's expectations of stoicism and strength. The decision came not from a place of defeat but from the understanding that to thrive genuinely, one must honour oneself above toxic expectations.

This book is a testament to that choice, a call to others to 'open the bleed off,' to release the pressure and prioritise oneself over the relentless demands of an often-heartless world. I encourage you to seek happiness through authenticity and empathy, to forge connections based on understanding and compassion, and to treasure the fragile, beautiful gift of life we all share.

We can redefine what it means to be 'strong,' replacing stoicism with openness and judgment with empathy. It is time to enter the sunshine of healthy living and working environments, where kindness and understanding are not signs of weakness but the most tremendous strength.

Remember, your well-being is not a luxury; it is a necessity. Life is too precious to be spent under the crushing weight of toxic expectations. Allow yourself the grace to prioritise your happiness to cultivate a rich life of empathy, understanding, and, most importantly, self-compassion. It is not just possible but essential for a life lived in pursuit of genuine happiness to feel genuinely experienced.

A WORLD THAT ISN'T OPEN

―――※―――

"When you lose your ego, you win. It really is that simple."
— Shannon L. Alder

Why Aren't We Opening Up?

Every great movement, organisation, or transformation begins with a powerful question: Why? In a world that often feels closed off, lonely, and sometimes scary, we must ask ourselves, "Why aren't we opening up?" This book aims to explore this question and offer insights into how we can foster openness and vulnerability in our personal and professional lives. From this exploration, I hope to provide a way through the many wounds we have been facing the last few years that have caused you to feel a rise in stress, fatigue, and a large amount of pressure in your life that has left you feeling isolated, lonely and even scared to ask for help.

Just as "Start With Why" delves into the significance of understanding the reasons behind your actions, "Open the Bleed Off" focuses on the transformative power of recognising your inherent value and embracing openness within yourself and others. The goal is not to dictate how to think or behave but to inspire a more open, connected way of living.

The stories and lessons shared in this book came from personal experiences in Oil and Gas and speaking to the energy industry about their struggles with mental health and the stress, pressure and burnout from years in this world. It also came from years of trying and struggling to grow a small brand and eventually reach a wide audience. I have drawn from my family life and shared some open wounds in the hope that vulnerability wins, and e shared some war stories, it might sound controversial, but life throws us moments and it's up to us to use them as we see fit. A few of them came to me from the most unlikely of sources. Scruffy drillers, soft hearted quiet men, and one that forced me to rethink my entire choices to work for people who are not in the same fight as myself. By revealing these stories with you of courage and vulnerability, I hope to ignite a spark within you and encourage you to embrace your light and openness.

I know it's a funny thing to consider, the fact that we must write books on this shit is beyond me. More than ever people are not concluding that we need gentler open-hearted communication but rather they are crumbling under the weight of worry and work never feeling the ease to reach out to someone or ask for help if they are having a troubling day as they fight for every hour to make it to shifts end. I know you know what I'm talking about. The pressure, like an invisible hyperbolic chamber wrapped around you and your friend's, all the while trying to play make believe that everything's fine. When in fact the pressure is so tight, so dense, it's a wonder you've not imploded from it. If you think I'm talking nonsense, just wait, as upsetting as it might be to hear, if it's not coming for you, it's coming for those you care about!

There is hope however and it's a strong hope. The principles of empathy, compassion, and openness are integral to creating lasting change. By integrating these values within your organisation and personal relationships, you can tap into the power of human connection and foster an environment that thrives on openness.

We won't dismiss the ongoing efforts to improve the workplace or diminish the value of existing trials and attempts. Instead, we'll focus on how to amplify the potential that already exists within you and your organisation. We all have this unspoken energy, and it's time we tapped into it. You can create transformative change by having the courage to ask for help and open the "bleed-off" in your life, business, and personal relationships.

The stories in this book are about individuals who have asked for help, found hope, and begun to heal. It's about how they've opened the "bleed off" and changed the reasons that prevent us from living in an open world. By asking for help! By embracing the principles of openness, we can create a world where vulnerability, empathy, and connection thrive.

Embracing the Unspoken Pain

The Hidden Struggles Behind Masculinity's Mask

In the quiet corners of our lives, away from the sparkle of social media and the demands of daily routines, we often bear a weight that goes unseen. The mask of masculinity can be both a shield and a burden, concealing the tumultuous storms that churn within us. This chapter doesn't aim to evoke pity or sorrow; instead, it's a beacon of candid truth, a testament to the transformative power of opening up.

Life, as we know it, isn't an endless stream of victories and triumphs. It's a tapestry woven with struggle, pain, and resilience threads. It's about meeting situations that leave us scarred, wiser, and sometimes shattered. I, for one, have danced with my share of adversity, and I share this not to paint a picture of despair but to illuminate the path of healing through speaking.

"Sometimes tears are a sign of unspoken happiness, and a smile is a sign of silent pain." - Unknown

In the past few years, I have stood by helplessly as four friends succumbed to the darkness of suicide. I've navigated the rough waters of divorce, seeing the toll it took on my son as he grappled with the upheaval. An accident nearly cost me my right hand, a career that once defined me evaporated, and the pandemic isolated me from the world, leaving me adrift for two long, isolating years. Loneliness, depression, and financial strain gradually eroded the edges of my mental fortress.

I recount these experiences not to evoke sympathy but to emphasise that life's struggles touch us all. You may carry a similar load or a unique blend of adversities. Regardless, there's one truth we all share: life's trials can accumulate, unseen and unheard, until they threaten to drown us.

Speaking about these struggles takes a lot of work. Society often celebrates stoicism, the art of keeping an unflinching facade. But the truth is, this illusion of strength comes at a cost. The real power lies in unveiling vulnerability, in recognising that asking for help is not a sign of weakness but a testament to our courage.

My journey through the labyrinth of life has revealed that speaking is healing. It doesn't obliterate the pain but breathes space into it, allowing the healing process to begin. We don't need elaborate rituals or grand gestures; the power lies in the simplicity of opening. I felt a shift within me when I started embracing the unspoken pain. I felt lighter inside like a door to clarity had opened to me. Sharing my struggles, even in fragments, felt like a profound release.

This chapter isn't about mere catharsis; it's about transformation. It's about the hidden crevices of pain that lodge within us, where the pressure mounts until we feel ready to burst. The key to unlocking this pressure is simple: it's your voice. I often wished for resilience to shield me from these challenges, but strength doesn't mean bearing it all alone.

The journey involves peeling back the layers of masculinity's mask, exposing the raw, unfiltered emotions beneath. It's about allowing yourself to be vulnerable, not wallowing in self-pity, but creating a healing space. This book is your guide to embracing your unspoken stress, to turning the valve of your bleed-off mechanism - your voice. By embarking on this journey, you're reclaiming your power, embracing your humanity, and stepping onto a path of profound transformation.

"It's so hard to forget pain but even harder to remember sweetness. We have no scar to show for happiness. We learn so little from peace."
— Chuck Palahniuk

I've been hiding from myself

This extract is from my LinkedIn post, which reached over one million.

For over two years, I've lived without my son. And it has broken me. I never told anyone last year when I cycled the NC500 what I was doing and why. Or the reason I stopped speaking, posting, and helping thousands of people with their mental help. After a string of powerful and moving collaborations, I was Invited into businesses and organisations to help men and women open up their unspoken wounds, which I did from the heart.

I fell apart in the quiet of my own home. I was secretly dealing with a harrowing issue, causing me to struggle so painfully that I pulled away from family and friends. I cried into the night, looking at empty messages without replies. One week became a month. Then, six months. Then, a year. It broke me. I begged, pleaded, and searched my soul to find a way. I was locked out. I have always inspired people to ask for help. I was at the end of my path when I broke down and cried like this. I honestly couldn't breathe without my son in my life.

Solitude became my ally. It became my final teacher, mentor, and guide. For six months, I sat curiously, listening to the agony I had held deep. And I reached out for help—more than twice. Therapy helped me feel the pain and what it was trying to give me.

Unmanifested Light.

I had deep, unresolved childhood trauma. I buried it so deep even I had locked it away. The knowledge of a lifetime of rejection made me strong and bold, but I had to surrender to my heart and realise I had something more to do for me.

Pain is a fire; it can be your road to ashes or the torch of hope. Hiding from yourself is what most of us do when we're hurting. The shame of not having my son around caused me to ignore my advice. Help thousands but not myself—the age-old self-reflective sabotage.

It's not a woe-is-me. It's WE NEED YOU!

They say men don't cry, but I learned it's okay to cry in the forces. We even have a name for it: " catharsis. "

#battlecry

I'm no longer at war with myself. My son came back to live with me on his own choice. I've been quietly writing my latest book and spending time with my boy, travelling and figuring out how to be a better father as he grows into a man father and son moment. I've cried, laughed, and let my heart open fully.

This is a battle cry for men to feel safe in this space and to be men who think and feel emotions. Who hurt? Who harbour pain and anguish. But knowing you are never alone. All you need is to know there are those of us who can hear a #battlecry and will come to your aid.

I am no longer ashamed of my wounds. They have given me a beautiful experience and meaning in this madness. This is me; this is my #battlecry, and I am proudly here to say that if soldiers and warriors can cry. All of us can.

This message is for you to heal and find hope. To feel safe amongst one, if not many. I will share the most intimate moments in the coming days and weeks. You're welcome to leave a reply and share this #battlecry

#mencry #anxiety #mentalhealth

When I wrote that post on LinkedIn, I was fighting a completely unrelenting battle during the pandemic. I had been alone for all of it. I had a few visits, but we all knew we had to avoid everyone. Locked inside and kept hidden from view. My world crumbled, and I couldn't take it anymore. Having missed my son for years, I couldn't hold on any longer. I published my pain into the void of social media, and I lost myself. I'd taken to hiding all my pain like most men often do. I masked it. I concealed it and held up a front that I was living quite well, but I fell apart in the offline modes behind my walls and eventually lost myself to the pain. It pushed me to open, and I let all the pressure pour out.

I never realised that nearly two million people would see my face cry. I also never expected those people to show me empathy and kindness. This experience changed my view forever on the stigma attached to men who are afraid to call out for help.

STRESS

"My body needs laughter as much as it needs tears. Both are cleansers of stress."

— Mahogany SilverRain, Ebony Encounters: A Trilogy of Erotic Tales

The Weight of the World - Where Stress Takes Hold

Don was a larger-than-life man with a fantastic job in oil and gas, filled with laughter and fun, and he had this way of making you feel better about yourself. Don always made your day feel easier whenever you had a problem at home. One time, I was going through a massive change, a divorce, and he was there for me. It helped keep me upbeat when my life was incredibly dark and stressful. The mad thing is Don was a six-foot-four mountain of a man. His patience and understanding were second to none—a genuine one in a million. One day, we were rigging down a large section of equipment from the drill floor, which was being lifted and backloaded using the platform crane to the boat and then sent back to the beach, a five-tonne piece of iron which assisted the drill pipe in the derrick, a pipe handler; we had to dismantle it section by section and lay it down horizontally to get prepped for the crane to lift it to the boat. The tool pusher in charge of us tasked me with securing it. Two others of the crew were putting on a set of slings, and a pulley system called a come along made a distinct cranking sound with each arm rotation. I used it to move the machine's main section across the racker's components. I started pulling on the come along, and the two crewmen shouted my name, "Stevie." they cried out to me with worry. I didn't reply; I just reacted. My legs jumped, and I sprung out of the way without looking to see what was happening. Call it gut instinct or second nature from having lived through enough dark times, but I knew not to waste time looking around for the danger.

When my feet hit the ground and I was out of the equipment area, I looked around. I watched the lower arm of the hydrocracker floating down about two meters a second. It came to a thumping stop, bumping into the stoppers at the end of the components. Nothing too dramatic at all, seeing this stuff is made of iron and steel. If they hadn't shouted at me, I would have lost my legs that day.

I looked up at them in shock. We all had a half-wry laugh and then did that double-take to see if any managers were around to see what had happened. No one was around, but I saw a large male head with a vast Harley Davidson handlebar moustache looking directly at me through the top of a container. I knew those eyes, and I knew that moustache. It was Don. He saw the whole thing.

I waited for the talking, too; he was the safety man. It's his job to ensure every detail of the work scope on the rig is to the safest possible standards, and without a doubt, he was the man for that job. But being Derrickman, I was about speed and accuracy, quickly getting the job done to the highest standard. Either way, I was now in the clutches of the Don. His eyes glued towards me like a thunderbolt from Zeus. "Oh, bollocks," I thought. Instead of coming at me with some policy or procedural nonsense, he just shook his head. He gave me a sideways smile that suggested I was lucky it was him and not the Tool pusher or OIM. Accidents happen; it's a busy, very manic place sometimes, especially during a rig down of the entire drilling package system. We had lost the contract to drill the oil wells, which meant the company had to remove the drilling package as the last well was a complete and total disaster, resulting in a well control situation that ended in a well kill operation taking three weeks to complete. Stress was at an all-time high, and things were moving fast daily. Don't let the incident slide. Not because he liked me but because that's what Don is like. A good man, he must have realised I had a lot on my mind. I was still stressing over the divorce and having to handle all the pressure of a team and overseeing lads while struggling to keep myself together.

He was like the father we all looked to while on the rig. He was a bloody good bloke, so I find it painful to share the story that Don sadly took his own life. Not while at home, he was offshore with all the lads and plunged into the dark of the North Sea in the middle of the night.

Writing this is hard enough, remembering the day I was phoned by one of our mates, John, while I was cooking spag bol in the kitchen as my son was in the living room playing PS4 and the phone buzzed.

"John, ya big baldy bastard, how the devil are ya pal."

"Stevie, have you heard about Don?"

"No, what's the daft bugger done now, smashed another motorbike into Tesco?"

"Mate, where are you?

"In the kitchen, why? What's this about John?"

"Steve, Don was fished out of the water a few hours ago; he's dead!"

"..............."

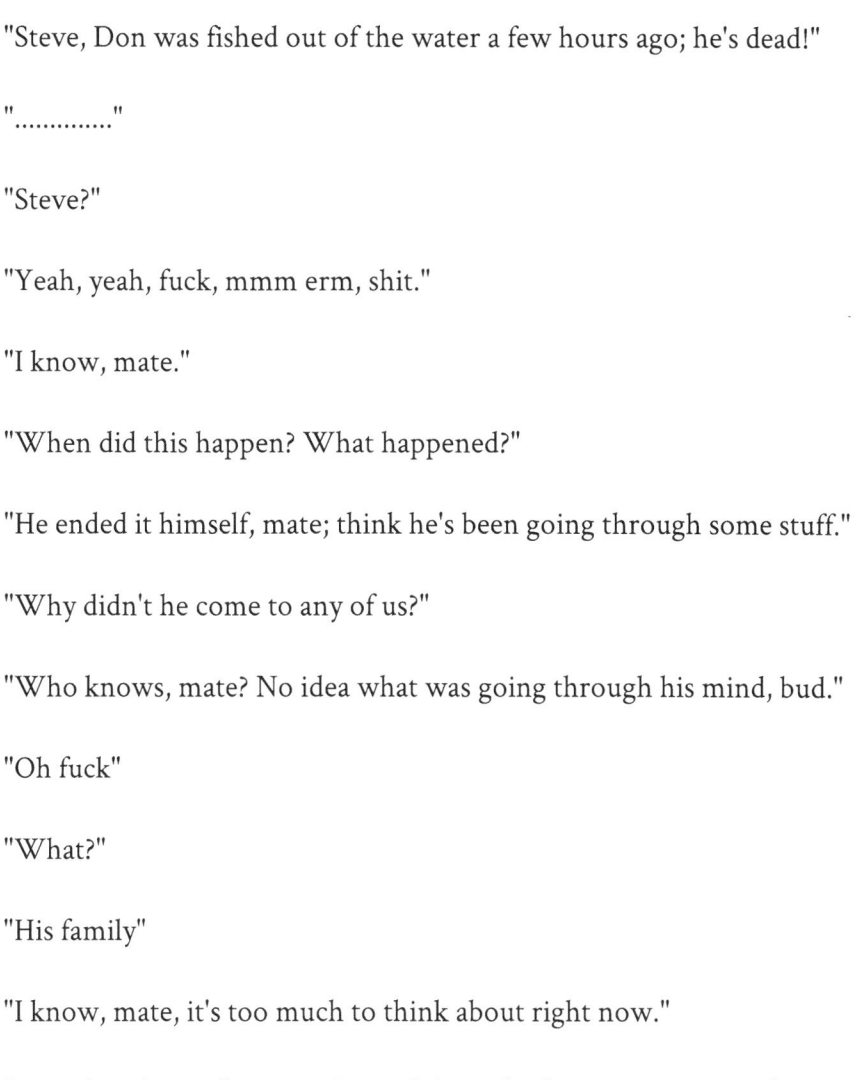

"Steve?"

"Yeah, yeah, fuck, mmm erm, shit."

"I know, mate."

"When did this happen? What happened?"

"He ended it himself, mate; think he's been going through some stuff."

"Why didn't he come to any of us?"

"Who knows, mate? No idea what was going through his mind, bud."

"Oh fuck"

"What?"

"His family"

"I know, mate, it's too much to think about right now."

I put the phone down and gazed into the living room, watching Jack playing PS4; he gave me the biggest smile. I smiled back at him, trying to conceal my pain and shock. I was holding back the tears, trying to put on a brave face. Then it hit me. It's what I always do. I keep it all bottled up, locked inside. I speak about mental health at conferences and events and help people. Still, when it comes to it, I'm so terrible at opening and letting people in and letting those close to me how I'm finding things hard that I am not some warrior with stoic stem cells for dealing with life. I am just a man. And I know it must have been the same for my friend. Unable to open up, unable to manage the pressure of life and work. Incapable of letting off some stress that has been building up for years. Afraid to speak up or let it out for fear of being ridiculed or laughed at, mocked or ignored and expected to continue. It's how it has been for decades in this Industry. We like to speak about being strong, disciplined, and driven by purpose. Where is humility, compassion, and empathy? The natural strengths of a good man?

I miss my friend; I miss his laugh and his eyes telling me I fucked up. What I wouldn't give to have another chance to have a fuck up and have his big daft Harley Davidson moustache glaring at me in disbelief.

Instead, I'm writing about my friend who took his own life. Who couldn't find the words or the way to reach out and ask for the one thing he needed more than ever? It's the one thing this book is about. The only thing that can make a real difference to you or anyone you work with or have in your life that matters to you. Asking for help.

I'd give anything to help a friend in need; it's aching to know I couldn't help Don. So many times, I've played the conversation I could have had with him, like he did with me. To be there with him in his darkest moments, offering him a shoulder to lean on or simply another chance to take the piss and see him smile. Sadly, and like many others, I can't be there. But I can try and help others, which is why I write this story. It's a call to ask of you, and please reach out and ask for help. In the next chapter, I will share one of the most courageous stories I have ever seen anyone share. I had the privilege of sitting down with a woman who knew Don better than anyone. Way better than any of us offshore ever knew him. She speaks of his attitude towards family and life and his larger-than-life passion for being a man of integrity. His daughter.

To hear this conversation, head over to my podcast. Enjoy a break from reading and learn from Caitlin herself as we discuss this wound and how she bravely opened up to help others through a crisis.

https://www.youtube.com/watch?v=91nSNDv71yU&t=2200s

If you're reading this the old-fashioned way, go to YouTube and search for WOUNDED PODCAST.

The Daughter of An Offshore Worker Opens Up

And Why Her Courage Helped Hundreds Reach Out and Begin Speaking of Their Trapped Grief.

CAITLIN: Dad, My first love, my forever hero.

Don, my father, was more than just a parent to me. He was my confidant, my best friend, and my role model. Our bond was unbreakable, and despite our occasional disagreements, our love for each other was unwavering. We often argued over trivial matters, each refusing to admit we were wrong. "I'm never wrong," we would jokingly say, our stubbornness bringing us closer together.

I vividly recall one incident when my brother Harry and I drove our mum up the wall while Dad was away offshore again. We were mischievous and rebellious, and when Dad called to scold us, we paid little attention. But when he finally returned home, we received the sternest of scoldings. I stood at the end of their bed, innocently asking, "When are you going back to work, Dad?" I did not understand my words' impact, but it hurt him deeply. Looking back, I cherish that memory and long for the opportunity to have him come home again, even if it means facing his fatherly wrath.

One memory that always makes me smile is when I was in labour with my son Freddie. On our way to the hospital, we quickly stopped at Tesco. While we were there, Dad discovered a bucket catching water from a leak in the roof. He grabbed it and began chasing me around the store, pretending he was catching my "waters." We laughed hysterically, causing quite a scene. Moments like these remind me of Dad's playful and mischievous nature.

There was a time when Dad was working on a rig, and there was a suspected gas leak. He had to wear a gas mask to ensure his safety, which meant shaving off his beloved Don Tash and beard. When I saw him without his facial hair, I barely recognised him. It was a comical sight, and I couldn't help but tease him, exclaiming, "That's not my dad!"

Despite his demanding offshore schedule, Dad made sure to be present for important family occasions. He would take us to school, cheer us on during sports days, and make up for missed birthdays and Christmases with the ones he could celebrate with us. He even attended behaviour meetings at school, showing his dedication to being an involved and supportive father.

Dad's opinion mattered more to me than anyone else's. I sought his guidance and valued his perspective on everything. Making him proud was always a driving force, and I constantly strived to achieve greatness in his eyes. Knowing that he was proud of me meant the world.

We shared many moments of escape from the realities of life. Whether it was embarking on long bike rides on his Harley, including the occasional heart-pumping encounter with the police for exceeding the speed limit or belting out carpool karaoke tunes to Nickelback on our way to visit Howie and Sandra (a private joke only we understood). We found solace in nature, away from the distractions of technology, in what Dad referred to as his "big green gym."

One of the deepest wounds is when I think of Freddie, the apple of my father's eye. Being a grandfather was Don's greatest treasure, and it hurts more than words can say that he won't be around to watch them grow into men. They only have a few moments of memory, but I hold these as beautiful and precious. You never know how long those you love will be around, and that time is so special and worth cherishing.

Freddie still asks for his granddad; Brodie never got to meet him. when we talk about my dad, they say, "Is Grandad in the sky?" Of course, this should be a sad time, and it often is, but I like to think of this as their way of moving through the wound—quite a gentle reminder of the resilience kids display. And yet, it's tender and sweet, knowing they still remember the way "grandad in the sky" means someone special.

It's both heart-warming and heart-wrenching to see my boys hold onto the memory of their granddad. They carry a piece of him within their innocent hearts, and that brings a sense of comfort amid the pain of loss. As they grow older, I'll share stories and memories of their beloved granddad, ensuring that he lives on in their hearts forever.

These memories and countless others bring a mixture of joy and longing. My father, Don, left an indelible mark on my life and the lives of all who knew him. His warmth, laughter, and unwavering love shaped me into who I am today. The pain of his absence is immense, but I hold onto these cherished memories as a testament to the incredible bond we shared. It's the strangest feeling writing this for a book. Knowing my dad won't be able to read it. But I know he is with us in spirit. Up there, looking down on me with that massive moustache and handlebar sideburns. I miss him. A lot of us do. But even if I wish he were here to laugh at me while I make a mistake or need him to console me after a drama, nothing hurts as much as knowing my dad won't be there to walk me down the aisle at my wedding. That, above all, hurts the most.

Sharing this deeply personal story about my father's suicide is challenging and healing. I'm not healed, but the weight of grief has softened slightly through writing and speaking about it. I'm not here to tell you what to do but to remind you of our limited time with our loved ones. Some, tragically, have even less. Mental health is not a phrase that resonated with me a few years ago, but now, having witnessed its devastating impact first hand, I know in my heart how important it is to have the courage to open up. We never know just how close someone is to the edge. So, let us have the compassion to lean in and listen. And when the time comes, offer a helping hand. It may just save a life. Since sitting down with Steve on his podcast "Wounded", I have realised that many more women like me have been holding their grief far too close. When the episode aired and hit social media, I thought a few people might hear it. I was astonished to see thousands began listening and opening to me about their trapped pressures and stress. I've never done anything like this before, and it proved that speaking about our wounds and opening up to others is the most beautiful thing we can do to express our grief. There's something special about being human. It reminds us to be gentle and kind to those going through the darkest times. And that this act alone is the most merciful of all traits. When we show compassion, empathy, and kindness to one another, it gives us back a little of that healing fire.

PART ONE

A WORKPLACE LACKING PURPOSE

> "Live the Life of Your Dreams: Be brave enough to live the life of your dreams according to your vision and purpose instead of the expectations and opinions of others."
> — Roy T. Bennett, The Light in the Heart

The Assumption of Understanding

In recent years, the phrase "mental health" has become a common buzzword, with people increasingly recognising the importance of caring for their mental well-being. However, the term only partially captures what we experience daily. A renowned public speaker and author, Simon Sinek, believes we should approach mental health with a sense of "mental fitness." He argues that just like our physical fitness, some days we feel strong and fit, while others we feel tired and drained. Mental fitness acknowledges that our mental well-being is not static but a continuous journey that requires effort and attention. Whether we call it mental health or mental fitness, what truly matters is having the courage to be open about our struggles and experiences. In this chapter, we will explore Sinek's thoughts on mental fitness and how it can help us navigate the ups and downs of life. I genuinely admire Sinek's views; his talks have changed me deeply.

How Are You Doing? People ask This simple question in passing, and the typical response is, "I'm good" or "I'm fine." It's usually returned with a "not bad" quite average British stiff upper lip response. But what if we stopped to consider the deeper meaning behind the question? What if you were honest about how you're feeling? Especially in the workplace where you spend a significant portion of your time?

In a recent interview, Sinek shared his experience of feeling at the end of the curve in his work, like he had reached his peak, and how he yearned to return to his untethered self. He wanted to be uncomfortable again, professionally. However, he also spoke about his feelings on mental health and why he felt the phrase "mental health" doesn't fit well. He believed it undermined the truth of what we experience daily at work, at home, and in our relationships. Instead, he suggested we approach the idea of our mental health with a sense of fitness.

I was at a conference in April of 2023 called "Mental Health in Energy", and the main speaker was a gentleman from the IADC (International Association of Drilling Contractors) called Darren Sutherland. His many years in the energy industry served as a touching and humbling vision of where we are today in the workplace and our mental health as an industry. As I sat in that conference, listening to Mr. Sutherland's words, it became even more clear that the traditional approach of looking at mental health in the workplace was no longer sufficient. Men and women felt the burden of pressure and stress, taking a toll on their mental well-being. While the oil and gas industry may have once embraced a rugged, masculine image, we can no longer ignore the changes in today's world. We've lost friends and colleagues to suicide, burnout, and mental illness; we can't afford to let this continue.

But it wasn't just Mr Sutherland's message that struck me that day. It was his approach. Rather than claiming all the answers, he invited us to create a movement, recognising that change begins with a collective effort. As I reflected on his words, I realised that the buzzwords we've become attached to, like "mental health, resilience, and passion", can sometimes be limiting. We need to recognise that the pressures of life ebb and flow and that we need to focus on our mental fitness in a broader sense.

For years, I have been sharing my story in public in the hopes I could help people gain a sense of control over their wounds. We all hold unspoken wounds that live within us. Our childhoods can hold us prisoner to the present unrelenting forces of invisible power that prevent us from moving forward. The pressure of a divorce infiltrates your work. Your loss of hope for yourself pushed you to the corner where you are boxed in and beaten hard. Unable to escape the hardship of depression can cause a storm of pain to crash into you every day before you leave the house. The pandemic may have unravelled you in a way you never saw coming. Maybe you've lost your passion for what once was a fulfilling career, but now it only brings you dread. A few people decide to leave the company, and without seeing it coming, the entire culture of that brand tilts in the wrong direction, causing you anxiety and stress as their values don't reflect your own. They make you second-guess your attitude towards the very thing you once loved.

It can begin with a single event that cascades into a personal hell that leaves you isolated and alone. Too afraid to ask for help for fear of seeming weak or pathetic. You could be stressing about telling your husband or wife as you've heard horror stories from friends whose relationships fell apart over fewer struggles. In short, this life can feel like a minefield, and there isn't any REAL help.

Today is when we are terrified to trust the media, afraid to believe in our government, and anxious to let our employers know we are struggling with mental health issues for fear of being set aside, let go or worse, Ignored.

After speaking to thousands of people in person about their mental health at work experiences, they are too scared to reach out, open up, or ask for help. We hold a very convoluted approach to understanding things that don't quite fit into the processes or policies that have been around for decades or even a few years. People are not systems. We are not procedures, and we are not policies. We are people. You have feelings, and this matters more than what some stupid poster at work might suggest, you know, the ones I'm talking about. The fake campaigns seem plastered around all the office boards that update everyone. These don't work. Can you imagine the Prime Minister having these in Downing Street? Or a General having these poster campaigns in the field of battle? They don't bloody work. We need to address the matter head-on and in a very human, practical way. What I'm trying to say is this:

You can't inspire a person to find purpose in their work with a poster or a policy that provides them with a phone call or a few sessions of occupational therapy. This department needs and deserves a set of standards that embody where the world is heading and where it is right now. It requires movement- a shift in perspective that signifies a real commitment to lasting change.

Words have power, and mental health is a term that has acquired considerable weight. But ultimately, it's about our human experience - the highs and lows, the joys and sorrows, the successes and failures. So, while the term "mental fitness" may be more appropriate, in the end, what matters most is our willingness to be open and honest about our struggles and our commitment to supporting one another through them.

It's time to start a movement. Or at least begin embracing a new way of asking for the help we need. Asking for help is one of the hardest things in the world for anyone to do, and this book's purpose is to open this idea up to see what we can collectively achieve for the betterment of all. I've been active in this in my work for over fifteen years. For the past five years, I have focused heavily on leading by example in my Industry. I have sat with hundreds of men and women in their place of work, sharing my story of anxiety, depression, and PTSD, and opened up to them authentically. I use profoundly passionate language (yeah, I swear at times) and address them without a single PowerPoint or slide. I engage with them at their level and do not expect anyone to be anything but themselves. After four years, I realised there was a way to take this to a deeper level and help people open the bleed-off in their lives by releasing some of that pressure. HOW? It's remarkable how simple life can be when facing a problem. All it takes is for one person to be humble and share their experience. We don't all have to be public speakers; you certainly don't need a college degree or certificate to do this. Wisdom is not unearthed from passive online courses. It is uncovered and shared through people opening up and being present with one another. Sharing stories, offering guidance and letting people come to their realisations. I'll share more on HOW this can happen later in the book.

Like our physical health, our mental health can fluctuate. Some days, we feel strong and fit, while others feel tired and drained. It's normal for our bodies to feel vibrant and pleasing one week and tired and achy the next. The body can also feel pain, and this is also normal. Sinek argued that mental health is a one-stop location, a finite approach. Instead, he proposed that we call it mental fitness.

He acknowledged that some days are good, great, and wonderful, while others are painful, hard, or just "Meh." He spoke about feeling lonely and how he used to suppress negative feelings. But during the COVID-19 pandemic, he learned how to manage his mental fitness as we had so much to deal with. He stopped hiding negative emotions and instead allowed himself to sit in them, to appreciate them as they made him more human.

Sinek even shared a moment of deep presence during a speech where he lost his train of thought, and his mind went blank in front of a significant audience. He realised that these moments of uncertainty and discomfort can be exciting, and we should let life fall into context, accepting that not everything will go to plan.

The workplace often needs more purpose, and we find ourselves going through the motions without direction or fulfilment. The assumption of understanding often leads us to believe that we are doing okay, even when we are not. In the next section, we will explore how the lack of purpose in the workplace can affect our mental fitness and why addressing this issue is crucial.

Purpose. It's such a buzzword and feels like it derives from the 80s or 90s with a Rocky montage needed to overcome the overwhelming odds faced in your life and work. The dictionary calls it the reason for which something is done. That is clear and makes sense, but it lacks that human element—the Why of the thing. For years, when I worked offshore in drilling, I never considered achieving the company goals as my own. Sorry to all the past clients, but I am just a man and have yet to embrace the culture of those crazy poster campaigns I saw hanging across the offices. For me, it's about putting my son's food on the table and seeing him happy on Christmas as he opens presents; it's about time spent with family and friends and enjoying my life. When I speak to the hundreds of men and women from my Industry, they all say the same thing. "I don't do this for the money; the time off keeps me here." That is a belief I have held myself. The weeks we spent offshore, sometimes months of super high stress and pressure, all made sense as soon as the helicopter landed on the runway, and we grasped that heavenly fresh air, that free air. Knowing our time at work was over for another month. But things have felt different lately. Even the time off is a struggle.

Life has become so fast paced and full of pressure that it's hard to find that off switch without something else coming to flick it back on. This constant on and off can lead to a sense of flux. You have so much change coming at you, pushing your control out of the way, making you feel out of control!

Control is an illusion, they say; I don't think this is true. You do have a measure of control over what happens in your life. Yes, you have no say over what other people and systems do, but when it comes to your daily life, there is a sincere level of control that you have management over. Chasing purpose or dreams can feel silly for us Brits; it's almost like we were born to get into work and stay with the same company. Yeah, that isn't what purpose is any more. And maybe we've all had too much of being told we need purpose. So what can we do? What can we aim for if not purpose? Before we find the answers, you look for, let's look at why motivation is a waste of your time.

Ineffective Workplace Motivation Tactics: Why They Fail to Inspire

Do you need help to motivate your employees, team, or colleagues and wondering why your tactics aren't producing the desired results?

Maybe you are done with how things have been so high-pressured and deeply stagnant where you are? Have you wanted to quit? Take a few weeks off? Or maybe you've arrived at the place where you lack the purpose to give a shit about work altogether?

Countless articles suggest various ways to boost employee engagement and productivity. However, most need to address the employee motivation strategies that do not work. Managers and executives must learn about effective motivational techniques and recognise and avoid ineffective ones. In this section, we will discuss some common tactics that may seem logical but demotivate employees.

As leaders (hint: if you're reading this, then you are a leader), it's our responsibility to motivate and inspire our employees. We spend countless hours searching for the latest strategies to keep our team members engaged and productive. However, the truth is that not all employee motivation tactics work.

Let's start with strict deadlines. While it's true that we all need to get work done on time, setting strict deadlines may only work for some. We need to remember that each employee has their own pace of work. Some may thrive under pressure, while others may crack. As leaders, we must know these differences and offer flexibility where necessary. Instead of focusing on the pace of work, we should emphasise the quality of the work produced.

I once had the privilege of sitting beside a wise, experienced man during a corporate event. We were trying to determine why employees kept leaving for our competitors, and he'd led several successful oil companies. In my youthful enthusiasm, I lamented my frustration with lazy employees and individuals lacking ambition. Having only recently left the military, I was still learning about leadership and management outside the military mindset.

To my surprise, this wise man shared with me a different perspective. He explained that a lazy person may be finding the most efficient and effective solution, the road less travelled. This was a pivotal moment for me, and it sparked a shift in my attitude towards my colleagues.

I learned that my earlier expectations and behaviours needed adjusting. While I still value hard work and productivity, I now approach my work with a greater appreciation for the different approaches and methods that people bring to the table. Through experience and reflection, I have understood that sometimes, the so-called "lazy" individuals may have valuable insights and solutions worth exploring.

Another ineffective motivation tactic is job status threats. Threatening an employee's job security can lead to disengagement and decreased productivity. When we use fear to motivate, we're essentially saying that we don't trust our employees to do their best work. Instead, we should focus on providing support and resources to help our employees improve. By investing in their growth, we can create a sense of loyalty and commitment to the organisation.

Co-dependent tactics, such as mandatory teamwork, can also backfire. While teamwork is essential for many projects, not all employees thrive in a group environment. Some employees prefer to work independently, allowing them to organise their thoughts and ideas without outside influence. As leaders, we need to provide our employees with the freedom to work in a way that suits them best.

Setting the bar too low can also lead to disengagement. When we don't challenge our employees, they become complacent and lose motivation. On the other hand, setting the bar too high can be unrealistic and lead to frustration and burnout. We need to find the right balance by setting challenging but achievable goals.

There are more, but these instil a sense of what we know works and doesn't. Each organisation is unique, but so are the people who work for them. The world has become so fast and stressful that it's worth taking a moment to strategically see where you are as a brand and decide which pathway is best for you.

In conclusion, we must be mindful of our motivation tactics as leaders. We should create a safe and supportive work environment fostering growth and development. Focusing on our employees' well-being and investing in their growth can inspire them to do their best work and create a culture of excellence. Remember, we can encourage our team members to be their best selves when we lead with empathy and compassion.

Managers need to prioritise the well-being and growth of their employees rather than solely focusing on productivity and profits.

Motivation strategies prioritising quality over speed can be more effective than strict deadlines.

Threatening job status as a means of motivation is demotivating and can lead to further disengagement.

While teamwork is essential, managers should recognise that only some employees want to work in a group and ensure that all employees are open to group projects.

Setting challenging goals can motivate employees to rise to the occasion, but managers should ensure they are realistic and achievable.

Managers should be open to trying new approaches.

Empathy, vulnerability, and authentic communication can help create an environment where employees feel seen, heard, and valued.

Managers can motivate employees to go above and beyond by fostering a sense of belonging and purpose.

Managers should strive to create a compassionate and understanding workplace that supports employees in their personal and professional growth.

REFLECTIONS

What happens when your world isn't open?

Individuals living in a world that isn't open may experience a range of negative consequences, which can significantly change their overall well-being and quality of life. Some of these consequences may include:

- **Isolation:** Without openness, people may struggle to connect with others and form meaningful relationships. They may feel isolated and lonely, which can worsen existing mental health issues or contribute to the development of new ones.

- **Suppressed emotions:** If individuals don't feel comfortable expressing their feelings and emotions, they may bury them, leading to increased stress, anxiety, and other mental health challenges. Suppressed emotions can manifest in symptoms such as headaches, muscle tension, or gastrointestinal issues.

- **Poor mental health:** A lack of openness can contribute to developing or worsening mental health conditions like depression, anxiety, and burnout. Individuals who don't feel safe or supported in sharing their struggles may find it difficult to access proper help and resources.

- **Hindered personal growth:** Unable to openly discuss thoughts, feelings, and experiences can limit personal growth and self-awareness. Openness is essential for learning, self-reflection, and development. Without it, individuals may struggle to recognise and address unique challenges or growth areas.

- **Reduced productivity and job satisfaction:** A closed environment in the workplace can lead to disengagement, reduced productivity, and low job satisfaction. Employees who don't feel they can openly communicate their concerns, ideas, or needs may become demotivated and less committed to their work.

- **Strained relationships:** In personal and professional relationships, a lack of openness can create misunderstandings, miscommunications, and conflict. Trust and emotional intimacy may be compromised, weakening connections and even breaking relationships.

- By promoting and fostering a more open world, individuals can benefit from improved mental health, stronger relationships, enhanced personal growth, and greater well-being.

HIGH PRESSURE BLOWOUT LOW PRESSURE LEAK

"Live the Life of Your Dreams: Be brave enough to live the life of your dreams according to your vision and purpose instead of the expectations and opinions of others."
— Roy T. Bennett, The Light in the Heart

Rockefeller Resilience – Mastering Stillness Under Pressure

How Stressed Are You?

Such a simple question, yet it carries a weight that can either uplift you, knowing you're managing life well, or drag you down, leaving you feeling overwhelmed by the daily grind. Stress affects us all differently, but recognizing how you handle it is crucial. Are you thriving, or are you struggling with the relentless demands of work, life, and obligations?

Consider this: are you facing a low-pressure leak or a high-pressure blowout? A low-pressure leak is the small but persistent stresses of everyday life—an unpaid bill, an annoying boss, or a frustration with a friend. These are the daily irritations that can slowly drain your energy and joy if not managed. Just like in the offshore sense a small leak is not something to start a silly panic over, but you do need to stop, take a moment and pay attention to it. Find out where the leak is coming from. Is it a wrongly closed valve or is there a seal damaged which needs replaced? These happen regularly and you won't feel much tension when they do but it's something you can't dismiss. Ignore it and it will come back to bite you in the backside.

In contrast, a high-pressure blowout signifies the major upheavals that can shake the very foundation of your life—a marriage breakdown, a betrayal, being cheated on, losing a loved one, or being made redundant. These events can feel catastrophic, overwhelming, and leave you questioning everything you thought you knew about your resilience. Like in real life a blowout is the worst event imaginable and when it happens to you there is nothing that can prepare you for it. All the lessons, teachings and stories from others will simply not do it justice. If it happens to you, it's blunt force trauma to your mind and body and the energy of this stress finds every fibre of your being. I wish there was a magic wand to wave away these moments, but life is life. When it happens. You can only navigate the pressure with the tools and resources you have. There isn't time to fuck around and find out. You must act with what you have. And under these circumstances you absolutely must trust in your resilience, or the price could be your life.

This chapter looks back at a man whose name is synonymous with resilience and determination—John D. Rockefeller. You might not agree with his methods or the cold demeanour some described, but his unyielding nature in the face of overwhelming odds offers lessons in a world that often feels intent on pushing us around. Let's dive into the essence of resilience.

The Making of a Titan

In the heart of the American industrial revolution, amid the clanging of iron and the roar of machinery, emerged a man who embodied an extraordinary sense of calm and resilience. Born on July 8, 1839, in Richford, New York, John Davidson Rockefeller's early life was anything but stable. His father, William "Devil Bill" Rockefeller, was a charismatic con artist, drifting from town to town, selling dubious cures and weaving tall tales. The family's stability rested on the shoulders of John's mother, Eliza, who instilled in her children the values of thriftiness, hard work, and self-control.

Young John embraced these lessons with fervour. By 12, he had saved $50 from raising turkeys and selling chocolates, which he loaned to a local farmer at 7% interest. This early lesson in investment planted the seeds of his future financial empire.

A Relentless Drive

In 1855, the Rockefeller family moved to Cleveland, Ohio, seeking a fresh start away from Devil Bill's scandals. At 16, John secured a job as an assistant bookkeeper at Hewitt & Tuttle, a produce brokerage. He was relentless in his pursuit of excellence, meticulously recording every penny in a journal he called Ledger A—a habit he maintained throughout his life.

His first job marked a turning point. "All my future seemed to hinge on that day," Rockefeller often recalled, celebrating "job day" every September 26. Dissatisfied with his low pay, he saved diligently and, by 18, opened his own produce brokerage firm. This venture thrived, cementing his reputation as a shrewd businessman.

The Oil Boom

The discovery of oil in Pennsylvania in 1859 ignited a frenzy. Rockefeller, sensing a golden opportunity, entered the oil refining business in 1863. Unlike the wildcatters who gambled on drilling, Rockefeller saw the real money in refining. His refinery in Cleveland was strategically located near new rail lines, ensuring efficient transportation.

Rockefeller's approach was calculated. He reinvested profits, expanded operations, and kept an iron grip on costs. By 1870, he founded Standard Oil, which swiftly grew through aggressive acquisitions. His tactics were ruthless, but they were driven by a vision of efficiency and scale. By 1882, Standard Oil controlled 90% of America's refineries, embodying the very essence of a monopoly.

The Weight of Wealth

Despite his ruthless business practices, Rockefeller's later years were marked by philanthropy. Having amassed immense wealth, he dedicated himself to giving back. He founded the University of Chicago and Spelman College and supported numerous medical and educational causes. His contributions to eradicating diseases like hookworm and yellow fever were groundbreaking.

Yet, Rockefeller's legacy is a study in contrasts. He was both a feared monopolist and a generous benefactor. His complex personality, marked by discipline, ruthlessness, and generosity, makes him a fascinating figure—one whose life offers profound lessons in resilience and the power of inner stillness.

Lessons in Resilience

John D. Rockefeller's story is a testament to the power of maintaining composure under pressure. His disciplined approach to business, strategic brilliance, and philanthropic efforts provide a roadmap for navigating modern life's stresses. Whether you're dealing with a low-pressure leak or a high-pressure blowout, the principles of resilience remain the same.

Rockefeller's life reminds us that true strength lies not in avoiding challenges but in facing and overcoming them with calm determination. In a world that often seems to have lost its grit, Rockefeller's legacy serves as a potent reminder that mastering inner stillness amidst external chaos is not just a skill but a path to unparalleled success and lasting impact.

As Rockefeller did, you will face many obstacles in your life. Some will come to appear as low-pressure leaks. Your wife asks you to mow the lawn right when the game starts; you've been waiting all week for this game and just wanted to sit down and enjoy it, so you are not in the mood for that task. Or your husband forgets to buy you a gift on Valentine's, and you put effort into the relationship lately; you took the time to get him a genuine gift, but you feel all your focus is being misplaced. There are so many of these low-pressure leaks happening. Life is leaky (ok, that is so corny, but you get what I mean). When you look back through the moments that have annoyed you, made you angry or upset, it's usually coming from a low-pressure leak that needs a little time and attention.

How you react is the baseline for resilience and fortitude. It's a simple way to see yourself. Do you respond to the everyday leaks with anger, annoyance, or frustration? You might do what many of us tend to: go quiet, ignore it, and hope things improve. Or can you change the flow?

Put your needs first and be the kind of person who realises others will not always prioritise your needs, and they will mess up and cause you stress. Knowing this can help you navigate the obstacles in your path. Until you genuinely feel a sense of self and see that life is a mass of leaky messes constantly appearing. You can begin to recognise that the obstacles in your path are the way through the path.

In the following segment, I have created a simple but effective tool to help you navigate those moments when those leaks appear and you feel overwhelmed and stressed. Life is packed of pressure, and this tool will act as a simple guide to help you navigate it when it happens.

The Pressure Management Tool. "PSI": Transforming Leaks into Resilience

Navigating life's pressures requires more than understanding; it demands practical tools that can be applied daily. Inspired by John D. Rockefeller's resilience and ability to maintain inner stillness, the Pressure Management Tool is designed to help you transform everyday stressors into opportunities for growth.

Step 1: Identify Your Pressure Points

Begin by distinguishing between low-pressure leaks and high-pressure blowouts in your life. Make a list of current stressors and categorise them:

- **Low-pressure leaks:** Minor but persistent irritations (e.g., unpaid bills, minor disagreements, work deadlines).

- **High-Pressure Blowouts:** Major life disruptions (e.g., relationship breakdowns, job loss, serious illness).

Step 2: Assess Your Reaction

Reflect on how you typically react to these stressors. Do you get frustrated and anxious or remain calm and composed? Understanding your natural response is crucial to developing better coping mechanisms.

Step 3: Develop Your Response Strategy

For each category, create a tailored response strategy:

Low Pressure Leaks:

- **Pause and Reflect:** When faced with minor stress, take a moment to pause. Practice deep breathing to centre yourself.

- **Prioritise and Act:** Determine if the issue needs immediate attention or can wait. Address what you can and let go of what you can't control.

- **Practice Gratitude:** Shift your focus by acknowledging something positive in your life. This helps keep perspective and reduce irritation.

High Pressure Blowouts:

- **Ground Yourself:** Grounding techniques (such as mindfulness or physical activity) can help stabilise your emotions in moments of major stress.

- **Seek Support:** Don't hesitate to contact friends, family, or professionals. Sharing your burden can provide relief and new perspectives.

- **Break Down the Problem:** Tackle the issue step-by-step rather than getting overwhelmed by its entirety. Focus on what you can manage today.

Step 4: Build Your Resilience Routine

Integrate resilience-building practices into your daily routine:

- **Journaling:** Like Rockefeller's Ledger A, keep a journal to track your thoughts, stressors, and responses. Reflecting on your entries can help you recognise patterns and growth.
- **Mindfulness and Meditation:** Regular mindfulness practices can help you maintain inner stillness amidst the chaos.
- **Physical Exercise:** Engage in regular physical activity to release stress and boost your mental well-being.
- **Continuous Learning:** Educate yourself on stress management techniques and apply new strategies as needed.

Step 5: Reflect and Adjust

Periodically review your list of stressors and your response strategies. Reflect on what has worked and hasn't, and adjust your approach accordingly. This ongoing process of self-assessment and adaptation is critical to building long-term resilience.

Applying the Tool in Real Life

Scenario: Low Pressure Leak

You have an annoying coworker who often disrupts your work. Instead of reacting with irritation:

1. **Pause and Reflect:** Take a deep breath and recognise the annoyance.

2. **Prioritise and Act:** Decide if addressing the coworker directly will help or if adjusting your workflow to minimise disruption is better.

3. **Practice Gratitude:** Remind yourself of a positive aspect of your job, shifting your focus away from the irritation.

Scenario: High-Pressure Blowout
You're facing a sudden job loss, creating financial and emotional strain.

1. **Ground Yourself:** Use mindfulness to calm immediate panic. Focus on the present moment.

2. **Seek Support:** Talk to family and friends for emotional support. Reach out to a career counsellor for professional guidance.

3. **Break Down the Problem:** Create a plan to manage finances short-term and begin a structured job search. Focus on one step at a time.

Conclusion

By naming stressors, assessing your reactions, developing tailored response strategies, and building resilience through daily practices, you can transform the pressures of life into opportunities for growth. The Pressure Management Tool, inspired by Rockefeller's resilience, empowers you to handle minor irritations and significant upheavals with grace and determination. Remember, true strength lies not in avoiding challenges but in facing and overcoming them with calm resolve.

Seeing the perspective, you need when the blowouts happen is often challenging. I have faced them many times, and when you are dealing with redundancy, it can force you to panic and worry when you have family and commitments to handle, such as mortgages and car payments. Will you manage to afford the holiday you've promised the kids? Can you still be seen as a provider? Will you find new work in time, or will this signify the end of the road as you approach fifty years old? Stress is stress. Blowouts happen. Nothing prepares you for it, and I hope to share this tool with you and the stories throughout this book to help you notice a straightforward and powerful truth. You are not alone. Even though it will feel this way, you are not alone in this fight. As a community of hard workers and managers, we need to stand by one another. Although it can feel like a dog-eat-dog place at times, we need each other, and this tool is a simple method to help you reach some clarity.

THE HIDDEN COSTS
OF A CLOSED WORLD

―――――※―――――

"The flow of spiritual connectedness and oneness with life will dwell in you
if your heart and mind is open and innocent."
— Bryant McGill, Simple Reminders:
Inspiration for Living Your Best Life

Why Openness Matters

In a world that thrives on connection and cooperation, seeing the consequences of a closed-off existence is alarming. As people, our innate desire to connect with others drives us to seek out meaningful relationships and experiences. And we need this more than ever in the workplace. Loneliness isn't simply a feeling you have on your own. Loneliness can settle in while you're around a dozen people five days a week or longer if you work in remote areas such as a drilling installation or a war zone. Being around people isn't the antidote to anxiety or loneliness. Having meaningful connections is what makes the experience matter.

We need people with empathy and compassion running our workforce. Now look. Suppose you wondered what is needed to win wars and defeat the enemy. In that case, you might be inclined to think it's savagery and brutality, but in truth, what matters most is not how quickly you pull the trigger. Still, when you make the brave decision "NOT TO," the reason I put war and soldiering in here is not because I served in a variety of warzones and operations at the most intense levels. It's because, for some reason, business uses vernacular references to war.

Mission statement: Get boots on the ground, set your sights, lay low, don't give up without a fight, don't lose ground, beware of a minefield, be your own worst enemy, expect casualties, and, above all, make a killing.

These don't exactly embrace you with compassion and empathy. Yes, businesses and brands need to add more value than their competitors to achieve financial success and create a strong culture of growth where everyone does well. But making a killing, taking no prisoners, and handling casualties are not inspiring or realistic. You wouldn't expect to fight a war with boardroom vernacular, would you?

"Davey hit those insurgents with some PowerPoint presentations and make them pay for what they did to Jonesy in that sales pitch. "

We must come together realistically, let some jargon drop a little, if not totally, and speak openly and plainly. That's why I've stuck to the simplest of speech to help us reach common sense and alignment. Jargon fills our minds with noise when we must focus on serving our hearts with a sense of collective empowerment and compassion.

Would you like to spend the next year or decade working with people you can't connect with or relate to? What would you do if faced with a genuine issue and you can't ask for help or some compassion? A value we need more of in the workplace.

When we lack openness, we can suffer adverse consequences that change our well-being and overall quality of life.

One of the most significant and detrimental consequences of a world that isn't open is isolation. With openness, people may find themselves able to form meaningful connections with others. This inability to forge strong relationships can lead to feelings of isolation and loneliness, which, in turn, can worsen existing mental health issues or contribute to the development of new ones. The pandemic forced us all into a world no one was ready for. Faced with vast lengths of time away from loved ones or regular exercise, we dealt with isolation collectively, and no one enjoyed it. I know none of us ever want that experience again. But loneliness still comes into our lives in a way that pulls us apart from the connective tissue of happiness; how a bully syphon a kid's joy over time in the school playground is the earliest version of this—having your trust and desire for pleasure taken away an inch at a time. Work can feel like this if we don't cultivate a culture of open-minded compassion and empathy.

When we think about the leaders we admire, they often have the ability to make genuine connections with those around them. They inspire trust, loyalty, and a sense of belonging by being open and transparent in their actions and communication. When we close ourselves to others, we inadvertently create barriers preventing these vital connections.

It's also hard sometimes to let down the barriers you've erected from years of effort to keep yourself safe and what may look like a successful climb in the corporate world. Imagine laying down the walls you've held up for so long and letting a friend inside your emotional centre feel like you're bearing your soul. The truth is less dramatic. In our efforts to begin opening up, I am going to share experiences in the coming chapters about what a real-time conversation and action look like from myself and a group of executives, working class, non-profits, and even the hardest of criminals can look like when YOU take the road of empathy, compassion and openness with the hope it can change the direction of your firm, brand and organisation for the better. This challenge isn't about changing the world. It's about changing the way we see the world we work in. It's not as big an idea as Martin Luther King once spoke of, but it is a small step in the right direction. And for now, that might be enough.

It's essential to recognise that the consequences of isolation are not limited to our personal lives. The ripple effect of a closed-off existence can also extend into our professional lives, hindering collaboration and teamwork. When employees are encouraged to be open and communicate freely with their colleagues, they are likelier to feel engaged, inspired, and committed to their work. In contrast, a lack of openness can lead to misunderstandings, resentment, and decreased overall job satisfaction.

As we strive to create a more open world in our personal and professional lives, we must consider how we can foster a culture of openness. By being open to new ideas, perspectives, and experiences, we can break down the barriers preventing us from forming deep connections. By embracing vulnerability and authentically sharing our thoughts, feelings, and experiences, we can create a world where isolation is no longer the norm but a distant memory.

In conclusion, it's crucial to recognise the power of openness in shaping our lives, personally and professionally. The consequences of a world that isn't open are far-reaching. They can negatively impact our well-being and quality of life. By embracing openness, we can counteract these effects and create a more connected, thriving world where people can come together and form meaningful relationships in and out of the workplace.

In the intricacies of life's tapestry, where threads of joy and sorrow are inseparably interwoven, there lies a profound truth often overlooked in the haste of our daily endeavours. This chapter, a mosaic of wisdom and vulnerability, reaches out to you in the gentlest way. Find the courage to lean into your softer undertones with the ferocity of hope that is needed in a world struggling for more light.

1. **In the Arena of Life, Vulnerability is the Gladiatorial Might:** The arena is vast, with many spectators. Yet, in the unveiling of your inner battles, the raw and unguarded moments where you finally open up, true courage is seen. Vulnerability, often mistaken for a chink in the armour, is, in fact, the very steel that forges the sword of strength. It's a silent pact of trust, extended outwards, that, in return, builds an unshakable fortress of collective resilience.

2. **Forge Bonds that Transcend the Superficial:** In the labyrinth of human connections, seek the threads that weave souls together beyond the superficial tapestry of physical coexistence. These threads spun from the yarn of empathy and understanding, hold power to transform a fleeting interaction into a sanctuary of shared existence, a haven from the relentless storm of life's trials and tribulations.

3. **Turn the Labyrinth of Jargon into the Path of Clarity:** In the world's grand stage, where words are often masked in complexity, dare to speak the language of the heart. Strip away the veneer of industry jargon to reveal the underlying human narrative. It's in

this clarity, this unspoken understanding, that ideas blossom, not just in the mind but in the soul.

4. **Be the Pebble that Ripples Empathy:** As a single pebble can disturb the still waters, creating ripples that reach far and wide, so can your openness. It's a gentle yet powerful force that sets into motion waves of empathy, understanding, and acceptance, reshaping not just your world but the world of everyone around you.

5. **In the Quest for Balance, Seek the Symphony of Existence:** The quest is not for a mere balancing act but for a symphony where each note, each beat, resonates with the rhythms of work, life, and the inner self. Acknowledge the cacophony of pressures, but also seek the quietude, the gentle pause between the notes, where the music of life truly unfolds.

6. **Let Empathy be the North Star in the Cosmos of Relationships:** In the vast cosmos where each star, each soul, is seemingly adrift, let empathy be your North Star. The light guides the force that draws one soul to another, not just in the gravity of understanding but in the orbit of shared humanity. In leadership, as in life, it ensures that every decision and action resonate with the mind's logic and the heart's wisdom.

In the following pages, these pearls of wisdom are not just words but invitations. Invitations to embark on a journey, not just outward but inward, into the very depths of the soul, where the most profound truths of existence await, ready to transform, ready to heal, ready to elevate.

STRETCHING AWAY FROM SHAME

"The flow of spiritual connectedness and oneness with life will dwell in you if your heart and mind is open and innocent."
— Bryant McGill, Simple Reminders:
Inspiration for Living Your Best Life

It's Scary Being Vulnerable

Ashamed, that's the feeling I had waking up on the stairs hungover after all my self-pity and hurt had burrowed so deep into my heart that I had ignored the basic human formula for growth. Taking care of yourself even when life is hard. Waking up in a mess was not a good moment for me; I'm sure you've found yourself in less-than-perfect situations, leaving you ashamed and scared of what others might think. We all do this. It's part of life's journey. But the feelings of shame don't come and go fleetingly like anger or jealousy; they sting deeper and cut like a jagged blade, leaving rivets across your skin that don't heal as smoothly as a clean cut.

But how could I become the sought-after speaker and consultant I'd been all these years? At least I was hoping to become better, I'd been putting in the effort and hours, but the world had turned to shit. COVID was in full swing, and my career offshore in drilling was down the drain. I couldn't even sign on the doll to get benefits as I had to eat up all my savings just to exist. Savings don't last long when you have zero income and no help from the government. It was a mess. I wish I had used that time to grow an online company and make a few extra thousand a month like others. Still, instead, I let the darkness come over me and empty my bank account, passion and purpose.

I was afraid and didn't want to open up or let anyone in. Why? It wasn't because I had no money or career; I had lost something far more precious. My son.

My boy and I have always been incredibly close, but after a brutal divorce and betrayal, I found my son changing and being more cold towards me; I tried everything to regain his old self and show him that nothing that happened between me and his mum caused me to love him or our relationship less, he was and is my most incredible light in the world. I was devoted to him, and he should know this.

My son became angry at me for reasons I can't explain, blaming me for so many lies and deceitful things that I could only let him grow through these feelings and come to his own choices.

I won't lie; this was the most challenging moment of my entire life. Seeing my beautiful boy hating on me and accusing me of things that simply were not true. I fell deep into a hole of self-loathing and drug-fuelled boozy months, and this lasted for a while. I sold my car, sold my items around the house and fell into a void of hurt and anguish. I lost connection to my boy. I had no idea this was an authentic experience, and they call it PAS or Parent Alienation Syndrome. I mean, I already survived PTSD and Depression, two wars and a divorce, and now this added pressure and right when I needed him the most, even just a phone call now and then would have been great. Nothing. I had no contact with him for years. I realised that in my self-pity and anguish, what I was truly feeling and experiencing was, in fact, grief. It was as if my son had been kidnapped, and all communication was gone. It was as if he was gone from me.

I'd lost so much of my time to mental health and PTSD from war. Then, I lost far too many friends to suicide. Now, after making it through all those horrible moments and hard times, here I was, alone, lonely and trying to get through two years of hell in a little council house all on my own. It's a grim moment. I was 39 and becoming a middle-aged, lonely single man. Without his son, no job, no avenue to focus on that would help me get out of this hell.

I needed a new way to see myself in this life. The scariest thing I held back from everyone during this time was not how unwell I was or that I was lonely. I had contemplated, for the second time in my life, to take it. I had no idea if I would make it through the journey. I didn't want to die. I didn't want to leave my son behind without speaking to him. I tried every day on the cycle to talk to him. Leaving hundreds of WhatsApp messages. Begging him to speak to me. I had not betrayed him; I was honourable to him and our family. Things had been brutal; surviving betrayal is a hard thing for a man to accept, but to then be driven away from the love of your child. Heartbreaking for anyone to live with. This was my darkest time. And in my own way, I opened myself up to the possibility of courage. I once heard that you don't get courage before the thing; it comes to you after you've been through it. So fuck it, I was going on an adventure.

Personal Struggle and Realisation

In the wake of my tumultuous divorce, the foundations of my world crumbled. Battling the demons of PTSD and depression forged in the fires of war, I faced a new, more personal battle: the alienation from my son. This estrangement was a byproduct of a bitter separation and a reflection of deeper emotional scars. As I grappled with this loss, I saw my son, my beacon of light, grow distant, his warmth replaced by a chilling coldness that pierced my already fragile heart.

Each day became a confrontation with my own vulnerabilities. I was no longer fighting the ghosts of my past but battling the essence of my present. My son's changing demeanour, a mirror to my internal turmoil, left me questioning my worth, not just as a father but as a human being. The betrayal I felt was not from him but from life itself, which seemed to strip away everything I held dear.

In those dark times, I sought solace in self-destructive habits. My descent into a vortex of drugs and alcohol was not just an escape but a cry for help that went unheard. I sold my possessions, piece by piece as if each item taken from my home tore a fragment from my soul. This was more than financial desperation; it was a manifestation of the inner void that consumed me.

Amidst this chaos, I faced a stark realisation: my struggle was not just about loss or addiction; it was about grief. The grief of losing a connection with my son was akin to mourning a living being. This revelation was both heartbreaking and enlightening. It marked the beginning of a transformative journey that required me to face my vulnerabilities head-on.

Facing and Overcoming Challenges

The road to recovery and self-discovery was fraught with obstacles. Recognising my vulnerabilities was one thing; confronting them was another. I realised that the path to reconnecting with my son and reclaiming my life was through healing myself first.

I embarked on a journey of self-reflection and therapy, unravelling layers of pain and trauma. This process was not just about recovering from addiction; it was about rediscovering my purpose and identity beyond the labels of 'veteran', 'divorcee', and 'father'.

As I healed, I began to understand the power of vulnerability. It became clear that my experiences were not just personal trials but universal challenges, particularly in high-stress industries like oil and gas. This realisation sparked a desire to use my story as a beacon for others, to show that even in our lowest moments, there is hope and an opportunity for growth.

This was a time when everyone was struggling; no doubt you will have faced your own nightmares and darker moments. I had an idea. Something came to me one day during this awful loneliness and estrangement. I knew that once in my life, I had unearthed the strength to face my demons head-on and placed my intentions again to do the same. I learned when I was battling my PTSD after four tours in a war that the only way, the only viable way for myself to face my demons was to meet myself and their head on instead of trying to medicate myself through them using prescription or over the counter drugs or alcohol or any other substance was to go charging like a mad man into the fires of hell that was the illness itself. PTSD, I realised, was not here to hurt me but rather to teach me. To open my heart to something more. To open the way to empathy. If I were ever to embrace this powerful and profoundly engaging emotion to learn its deeper purpose and to use it to help others, I would first have to embrace it fully myself. This meant learning to forgive my misgivings, accept my failures, and witness the true reflection of all my choices that led me to this place.

Overcoming my own PTSD was an experience I am so grateful I journeyed through. The wound had to become my way. And it did. I just never expected to have to face something even more terrifying. But here I was, about to embark on a soul-searching voyage that would begin at 6am on the 24th of August 2020. At the height of the pandemic, during sunrise to wake the gods, I set off on a bike that a dear veteran of the army gifted me from Twitter, who had lovingly sent it to me via courier without ever having met each other. So that I could cycle the NC500 route alone and discover something new from within myself in the hopes that I could heal. I opened to nature and allowed her to show me my weaknesses and flaws. I could hear my father's words from when I was a teenager in my first warzone, over an encrypted network satphone; he told me, "Know your friends." These words would become wisdom to me later on. And I need this more than ever now.

I set off at 6am, completely sober and fully embraced in the now, to cycle every single day for a month, all on my own, without anyone beside me. My thoughts, hopes, pain, suffering and loneliness would accompany the journey.

I slept on beaches, on the side of the road, atop mountains and rivers, and in fields. I enjoyed stormy weather, rainy days, sunshine, and beautiful landscapes that lifted me from agony and suffering. This was the greatest gift I have ever given myself, and each day brought me closer to myself; my feelings began to open up to me. I heard my own voice in my head speaking to me as if to say. Get up, get going, get busy living and sharing your story. One pedal at a time, one sweaty, achingly painful wheel cycle after another, I found my way across the glens and pathways of Scotland's most spectacular views. And here I was, often alone for days without seeing anyone. The longest I was alone was four days without seeing a soul. Occasionally, I would speak to a quiet old man sitting outside his porch or a deer I saw atop the hills during a rainfall. The rivers and lochs were as beautiful as my dreams. I felt connected to something more than myself; I felt the pain and hurt fade away as I learned to forgive myself for the grief that was within me. Grief disconnects you from the destiny you are here to uncover; it does not simply wait for you to have it handed to you in some way; you have to earn it, and making value is hard.

Relevance to the Oil and Gas Industry

Much like my journey, the oil and gas industry is no stranger to adversity and the need for resilience. The pressures of this field can often lead to a culture where vulnerability is seen as a weakness. However, my story underscores the importance of emotional intelligence and empathy in such environments.

Embracing our vulnerabilities can lead to a more supportive and understanding workplace. It fosters a culture where mental health is prioritised, and personal struggles are recognised as part of the human experience. This shift is crucial in an industry often characterised by rigidity and toughness.

Conclusion: Embracing Vulnerability

Reflecting on my journey, I see a path marked by pain and incredible growth and learning. At 39, standing at the crossroads of despair and hope, I chose the latter. This choice was not just for myself but for my son and for everyone who has ever felt lost in the shadows of their struggles.

My story is a testament to the power of vulnerability. It's a call to action for the oil and gas industry, and indeed for all of us, to embrace our human frailties. In doing so, we can transform our personal and professional lives, creating environments where empathy, understanding, and resilience are ideals and realities.

Conclusion: The Courage to Embrace Vulnerability

1. **Understanding the Power of Vulnerability:** Your journey teaches us that vulnerability is not just about opening up about our struggles; it's about confronting them, understanding them, and learning to grow through them. This message is particularly potent for those in high-stress environments like the oil and gas industry, banking and finance, engineering, education, media, and the press, where showing vulnerability is often seen as a weakness. It is, in fact, a strength.

2. **Resilience in the Face of Adversity:** Your battle with PTSD, the pain of parental alienation, and your fight against self-destructive habits illustrate a profound resilience. It's a lesson to face your deepest fears and emerge stronger. With its unique challenges, the oil and gas industry requires such resilience – physically, emotionally, and mentally.

3. **The Transformative Power of Nature and Self-Reflection:** Your solo journey, cycling across Scotland, reflects the healing power of nature and solitude. It reminds us of the importance of self-reflection, connecting with ourselves and our surroundings, and finding peace and clarity.

4. **Empathy and Emotional Intelligence:** Your experiences highlight the need for empathy and emotional intelligence, both personally and in the workplace. In industries known for their toughness, like oil and gas, fostering a culture of understanding and support can be revolutionary. It can lead to a healthier, more productive, and more fulfilling work environment.

5. **The Journey Towards Emotional Healing:** Your story is about the hardships and the journey towards emotional healing. It shows that recovery is possible, no matter how daunting the path may seem. This is a powerful message for anyone struggling with their mental health, offering hope and a way forward.

6. **A Call to Action for Personal Growth:** Your story is a call to action. It encourages us to face our inner demons, to embrace our vulnerabilities, and to see them as opportunities for growth and transformation. This message is especially crucial for oil and gas industry employees who often face extreme stress and pressure.

In conclusion, your story is a beacon of hope and a guide to resilience. It shows us that there is a path to light and healing even in our darkest hours. As we embrace our vulnerabilities and face our challenges head-on, we open ourselves up to a world of growth, understanding, and profound personal transformation. This chapter is not just a story; it's a roadmap for anyone looking to overcome adversity and find strength in their vulnerability.

PART TWO

A NEW APPROACH TO MENTAL HEALTH IN THE WORKPLACE

> "Nature is medicinal; the sun, large bodies of water, and deep breaths of fresh air. Healing is found in the mountains, amidst a forest, by fire, and water. I still recall how healing it was to be home, my parents' island, waking up to tropical sounds of morning; monkeys, tropical birds, and tropical animals discussing their days, feet in sand, and the glorious sound of tropical rain. Visuals of lush greens and vibrant flowers, nature calls us into ourselves, nature calls us home"
> — Cheyanne Ratnam

The Connection Between Purpose and Mental Health at Work

In the pursuit of creating a thriving workplace, the link between purpose and mental health appears as a vital cornerstone. When individuals have a clear sense of purpose and feel connected to the greater mission of their organisation, their mental well-being flourishes. A strong sense of purpose provides a framework that imbues even the most mundane tasks with meaning, empowering employees to find fulfilment in their daily endeavours. Now, if you are a simple bloke (like me) and you're stuck offshore right now. You have a mountain of thoughts to climb, a family to worry over, and a new team that lacks the experience you are used to.

You notice that the feeling could be better amongst the people you oversee. Try this.

Be the one to open first; share a story about when you felt you had no control over how things were going for you and were struggling with leaving your family behind. Let them know that you are not just a driller, manager, or leader; you are a man with feelings and have people you care about who need you to be at the top of your game. To do these things, you would respect the men and women of your crew to reach out to you if they are struggling. They don't always have to "open up" publicly. As we all know, crowds can be cruel, even if they only mean it in jest. But coming from you, the leader, it might have the right effect you hope to achieve.

This works because, as a detachment commander in the army, I would reach out to the young recruits who turned up on camp and make them feel welcome and safe. I ensured that my presence was always available to them, whatever they might need it for. When you work with a group of men, and they are away from loved ones and family, it's up to us as leaders to let them know we are there for them. Whatever that might look like. This was back in the early 2000s when I'd never heard of empathy and compassion in the workplace. Still, I knew I wanted my mates and team members who might need to rely on me for life-or-death situations to know they could count on me for anything. It's a straightforward and effective method of letting them know that we all have unspoken stress to handle, but if they have someone to help them, it's shared stress, which has a much better chance of being handled together than alone. Try it out; you might just be shocked at the results.

A lack of purpose can lead to a profound disconnection and disengagement. Employees may grapple with feelings of aimlessness, experiencing the weight of monotony and boredom. Such an environment can pave the way for stress, anxiety, and burnout, chipping away at the mental health of individuals within the organisation. It will also bring them closer together when they feel they can approach you without being made to feel stupid or worthless. It can feel strange to be with, but you are the one they need to come to if they have to head to another department because your team thought they had nowhere to turn. You will likely feel responsible, and they will not feel like a team. This is why companies need help to keep great people. Yes, the competition is fierce these days, and people love to make more money and have a new challenge, but it comes down to one simple fact. People leave because of people they don't get on with, like, or trust. It's not because they don't enjoy their work.

Cultivating Empathy in the Workplace

Empathy, the ability to understand and share another person's feelings, forms the bedrock of a compassionate and supportive workplace culture. Organisations foster an atmosphere of understanding and acceptance by encouraging empathy among team members. Employees feel valued, seen, and heard, knowing their experiences and emotions matter.

Leaders play a pivotal role in nurturing empathy within their teams. By setting the example of active listening and genuine concern for others, leaders create a safe space for vulnerability and open communication. When employees feel comfortable sharing their challenges, both personal and professional, they are more likely to seek help when needed and less likely to suffer in silence.

Compassion as a Guiding Principle

Compassion is the empathetic response in action. It involves understanding someone else's struggles and taking proactive steps to support and uplift them. In the workplace, compassion means extending a helping hand to a colleague in need, helping without judgment or expectation of return. A compassionate work environment is one where colleagues lift each other rather than tear each other down. It is a space where mistakes, which happen, can be made. Meeting them as such can become opportunities for growth rather than harsh criticism. When compassion thrives, employees feel a sense of camaraderie and unity, knowing they can rely on one another for support.

Embracing Each Other's Failings

In pursuing perfection, many workplaces inadvertently foster a culture of fear, where mistakes are stigmatised and seen as a sign of weakness. This approach stifles innovation and prevents employees from taking risks and exploring their full potential. In contrast, a workplace that embraces each other's failings as opportunities for growth cultivates a growth mindset. Leaders must create an atmosphere where failures are seen as steppingstones, not stumbling blocks. Encouraging individuals to share their lessons from setbacks fosters a culture of learning and improvement. When employees know that missteps are no longer punished but understood, they are more likely to take ownership of their growth journey.

The Unspoken Method: Creating a Supportive Ecosystem

The Unspoken Method champions the power of authentic connections in the workplace. It emphasises the importance of embracing vulnerability and seeking help when needed. Organisations tap into the strength of their collective spirit by creating a supportive environment where people can openly share their struggles and triumphs.

In the past, we have spent decades moving up the corporate ladder of industry and work by showing the rigid attitudes of stone, which reflect the time needed. The problem is we have stayed on this course as millions of brands stuck to this attitude as it worked for them. Profits soar, and people crash. You only need to look at the rising cost of lost time, which is upwards of £100b in the UK alone, from people taking time off due to stress, mental health, breakdowns and the pressures of the world pushing us into the corners of life we don't wish to be. This push comes down to ego—a way of looking at ourselves which can't be how we see ourselves anymore. The weakness is not in staying silent. The weakness is never sharing the stress you have held in for all this time.

As individuals, we must recognise that seeking help is not a sign of weakness but a testament to our courage and self-awareness. By being open about our challenges, we break down the barriers that separate us and forge a path toward true collaboration and empowerment.

In the following chapters, we will explore practical strategies for implementing the Unspoken Method in the workplace. From fostering authentic connections to championing empathy and compassion, we will unlock this approach's transformative potential. Together, we can reshape the landscape of workplace mental health, creating environments where individuals thrive, grow, and find profound fulfilment in their personal and professional lives. Men in traditionally masculine work environments often feel pressure to be tough, assertive, and unemotional. However, this approach can lead to a lack of empathy and compassion towards colleagues and clients, ultimately hindering success. By embracing emotional intelligence and vulnerability, men can create a more open, collaborative work environment that fosters better relationships and increased productivity. Organisations can play a critical role in promoting a culture of empathy and compassion by offering training, encouraging open communication, and recognising the benefits of a more emotionally intelligent workforce. It's time for men to realise that empathy and compassion are not weaknesses but strengths that can drive success in the workplace. How can men balance the need to be assertive and confident with the desire to be empathetic and compassionate?

What are some practical ways for men in masculine workplaces to show vulnerability without being seen as weak?

How can a more empathetic and compassionate approach benefit men in leadership positions?

What role does emotional intelligence play in helping men navigate a masculine work environment with empathy and compassion?

How can organisations promote a culture of empathy and compassion among men without sacrificing productivity or competitiveness?

These are some of the questions I have asked myself across two decades. It could be over thirty years if I included my military experience. Why do

I feel this way? Why would a man who served in wars and the most masculine of environments offshore (drill crew) be inclined to hope for a better model of how we seek to change the culture of masculinity in the workforce?

I have a story to share that shaped this side of me.

During a convoy in Kosovo, my nineteenth year around the sun, I ended my second tour of duty, helping to stabilise the peacekeeping mission the allied forces and NATO had tasked with us. We achieved this phenomenally, as the country has been stable since we arrived. It was a brutal engagement and the most significant turning point in my teenage years.

I was part of a team preparing vehicles for backloading to Germany. A small convoy, around five vehicles and only a troop of men, around 12 of us; the sun was beating down, it was a beautiful day, and our hopes were high as we were due to head home to Germany, where our post was. I had saved up a staggering four grand and was ready to party hard in the city once back in Deutschland.

The convoy stopped suddenly out of nowhere, and we all knew something was wrong. It's not like you get some sign or something silly, like a poster with a headline telling you it's about to get nasty. It's like a shift in how you feel. A sense of dread inside your gut that doesn't feel right. We all get this, and I'm not unique in this. Still, knowing what I know now, I am sensitive to change and emotional patterns in situations. It could be a survival mechanism. Who cares. I know I was unhappy with this stop.

I saw the man coming about twenty feet away, carrying something in his arms. His hands had a tight grip on this object. No, no, it wasn't an object. It wasn't something; it was someone.

As he moved closer, I could see what it was—a child, a young boy around twelve, maybe younger.

As the man approached, I could see in full detail the brevity of the situation. The kid wasn't moving, he wasn't screaming. He was dead. He'd stepped on a landmine or IED of some making, and his legs were mangled and ripped open. The blood had poured out, leaving only a dusty strewn of messed-up veins and tissue. The congealed blood had gathered around his knees, what was left of them anyway. His eyes were open and lifeless. The kid was murdered in cold blood by those who hid in the hills far from the scene. Whoever laid that device wasn't there to see the nightmare it left. I wanted to help, to give some aid to this moment. As those thoughts entered my mind, his mother entered the arena. Her screams were like nothing I had ever heard. Utter loss, moaning like a wolf tearing at the grief of losing its world, as if the moon had been stolen from her wild, free heart, leaving her void. It was both terrifying and caused me to freeze. I felt stuck in the horror of what this looked like and my inability to fix it.

I knew I had to do something, anything, to help them. Futile as it might seem, it's in our nature to aid those in need, and it's what honour stands for. I want to help those less fortunate and weaker than us by ensuring they feel safe and matter.

We got the order to leave them at the side of the road, jumped back into our vehicles and drove off. Never to see them again. As they grew smaller in the mirror and my mind raced with rage and disbelief, I realised I had no control over my life or my need to help others.

Years later, I would speak on large stages amongst government, politicians, financial brands, huge non-profits and across the media, sharing a lesson I had been given that day in Kosovo.

You can follow the rules of life or the ethics in your heart. That day, I followed life's orders and rules, costing me more than I could ever hope to pay. These days, I have come close to making the same mistake, but I have never done so. It has cost me hundreds of thousands in lost revenue or salaries to choose my heart's need to help instead of making money. But one thing is for sure. We live in a time that needs more people to choose ethics and ignore so many insidious rules—a choice we all must eventually make. Uphold the law, always, even though they too can feel challenging to adhere to given the injustices happening in recent times. But uphold we must. Rules, though, are there to be bent; some are fun to break. But never ignore the ethics of the times you find yourself in. There is more at play than making some money.

I am writing this to you because I was miserable and had to leave a career focused on bottom-line revenue and profit over the hearts of men. I know that profits matter, I care about making a few quid here and there, and the thought of a million feels excellent. If that is in the cards, then fantastic. But never at the expense of my honour and peace of mind. I'd rather be a happy, relaxed basic earner than a stressed-out running around building someone else's dream than to see my health risked again.

I'm not here to tell you which side of that coin to live your life from. I'm just here to remind us all that life doesn't have to be so absolute.

The Unspoken moments that shape you.

It's not easy talking about the moments from your life that you would rather hold in the quiet corners for no one to see or learn about you. I know because I held mine prisoner for years. That day in Kosovo was unspoken for over a decade, and it took me to the edges of my health before life itself pushed me over the cliff edge and forced me to face my demons. Depression and anxiety were the precursors to me opening up about my PTSD and the darkness that kept me fastened to my fear for so long. I forgot who I was. I pushed myself to work harder and harder until my heart forced me to leave. And I don't mean this figuratively; I mean it literally. I was sent home from a trip offshore due to my blood pressure becoming so high it was through the recognised roof of hypertension. The recording was 210/160 and climbing. I felt fine. That's what I told the medic. Who was on the phone at the beach (onshore offices) ordering me a chopper to get to the docs for a check-up and health review?

I knew it was more than work. It was a culmination of many factors. It was all the unspoken feelings, emotions, pain, hurt, frustration, and so many losses across years of never letting it find a bleed path. My body was forcing me to release pressure and find a way to calm down. Either that or I was about to implode from all the stress I'd stored. I later discovered that stress finds a way inside you and burrows deep into the bone and marrow until it finds a way out. The crazy thing about being a man is that we believe we are here to hold up everything, and admitting any pain is a weakness. Only pussies talk about mental health, they say. And there's one thing us lads hate. Being thought of as a pussy. Being looked upon by other men as weak, soft, unable to handle shit, be ready to tackle stress like a machine. We are not machines even if some think we should be able to push forward in every single facet of life without ever feeling stress, worry, fatigue, hurt, or pain; it's all part of being alive and being involved in work.

Things get messy, and they will push you around. There's a great line from a movie: "The world breaks everyone, and those who don't break, it kills, eventually" And I know this to be true. When I was young and enjoying being a soldier, I felt invincible and ready for action at any second. Now, in my Fortys, I am less prepared to charge into the battles of everyday life. I'd rather enjoy laughter, love, hope, calmness, and a sunny blue afternoon with a few beers and some great friends. I'd choose coffee and croissants in a chilled cafe with a good book over a mad dash office environment any day. I'm much happier in my middle age than ever, running around life like a lunatic trying to make the world happier; I'm just enjoying being here with those I care about and attempting to create a small change when possible.

Summary: Relevance to the Oil and Gas Industry of "A New Approach to Mental Health in the Workforce"

The insights from "A New Approach to Mental Health in the Workforce" are particularly pertinent to the oil and gas industry, an arena often fraught with high stress and physically demanding work conditions. The chapter's focus on the intrinsic link between purpose and mental health is crucial for this sector, where work can sometimes seem disconnected from personal aspirations and broader organisational goals. Embedding a sense of purpose within the workforce is critical to enhancing mental well-being and job satisfaction.

In the oil and gas industry, empathy and compassion in the workplace take on added significance. Much of the work's remote and hazardous nature can engender feelings of isolation and heightened stress. Cultivating a culture of empathy is essential, where employees feel their experiences and emotions are understood and valued. Leaders who practice active listening and genuine concern can create a safer space for open communication, which is vital in an environment where key people in charge may otherwise overlook mental health issues.

Furthermore, the chapter underscores the importance of reframing failures as opportunities for learning and growth, a critical mindset in an industry where risk management and safety are paramount encouraging a culture that views mistakes as valuable learning experiences can contribute significantly to personal development, operational safety, and innovation.

Conclusion

"A New Approach to Mental Health in the Workforce" provides a roadmap for fostering a healthier, more empathetic, and supportive work environment, especially relevant to the high-pressure context of the oil and gas industry. The chapter emphasises the need to intertwine an employees' sense of purpose with their work, promote empathy and compassion among colleagues and leaders, and view failures as growth opportunities.

Implementing these principles is more than a policy shift; it's a fundamental cultural change towards valuing and supporting mental health in the workplace. For the oil and gas industry, this approach not only bolsters the well-being of its workforce but also enhances overall productivity, safety, and innovation. This chapter is a practical guide and an inspiring call to action for organisations committed to making a meaningful difference in supporting their employees' mental health and well-being.

MAKING THE CONNECTION

Genius is the ability to put into effect what is on your mind
- F Scott Fitzgerald

Coming full circle in oil and gas and why completions gave me a critical insight into well-being at work.

Fortitude On the Forties

"Stevie, Oi Steeevie", Scouse shouted over the drillers squawk box from his cosy warm doghouse as we were racking back the warm wet drill pipe after drilling the last section of well before we got rigged up and ready for running casing.

"Stevie", Scouse blasted my ears again right after the five-and-a-half-inch drill pipe stand was pushed back by our hands into the deck, clanging into the rows of iron I'd been used to handling as the lead hand on the crew of roughnecks. I smiled at him as I knew some classic derogatory hint at my mum's weight or my dad's best mate Leeroy was at home keeping my missus happy and slippers warm.

"Stevie, oi, Steeeevie! " he shouted, and I turned and gave a wry smile. Scouse laughed; he knew he had me.

"Stevie, I wish I was your Daddy," he said in pure scouser fashion. I stopped and chuckled, then turned towards the doghouse in the middle of the night shift and spoke.

"Go on then, mate, ha-ha. Why?"

"Cos if I were your daddy, you wouldn't be so f&*%ki$ ugly." From the squawk box in his rich scouse accent, which gave his joke a punchier delivery. The whole crew laughed, and I just pissed myself at his humour. I knew I was at home and felt safe in this crew.

"Aye nae bother Scouse, you can be my daddy just as long as I can take your daughter out for the weekend", I jibbed back.

Scouse laughed, and we racked back the next stand of drill pipe into the derrick, setting it down safely and feeling like I was part of a great bunch of lads. The kind of men you can rely on. Not because they are perfect or never say the wrong thing. They just took the piss constantly, and we always got the work done safely and on time. We never hurt each other, and it was usually a state of flow on our crew. We had over a year under our belt working together, which opened the doors to know each other well. Our relationships ran as deep as the wells we drilled, and as much as they took the piss, they held with a degree of integrity I still hold dear long after we worked as a crew. We have trusted one another. Even when solid arguments and angry words were shared between us when stressed, or we acted out of line. We never crossed that line. We acted like men.

We had this sense of belonging. Without a doubt, there were moments when we fell out. Sparks flew, and it was funny at times and serious at others, but we always had each other's backs. We had the trust and muscle memory of each other's movements. We had flow and focus. We also had humour, a crucial ingredient for any working crew. We expressed empathy for each other during the challenges at home, from pregnancy issues, breakups, divorce, kids missing us or struggling with loneliness, money, and even losing friends in accidents or worse. We were less like a crew and more like a small working-class family who ran at the industry's highest level.

When you switch on your lights, fuel up your car or motorbike, have items delivered to your home from Amazon, or email and reply to mates or family on social media. We are the ragtag crews of the North Sea and energy industry across the globe that dare to step onto a helicopter every month, even when there is a risk to life each time. Or insane winter conditions that batter your soul for weeks through the darkness in the cold winter months. Battling the ferocious storms, the sea churns at you as you throw in the drill pipe with the biting wind slicing your face. We are the men and women who stand side by side and perform the highest-grade energy services that provide you with the comfort and care you take for granted. We are the scruffiest, roughest, hot-headed, and quiet ragtag men willing to stand in the dirt, grease, grime and oil with a face full of muck to bring our families and loved ones a great way of life. We are the women who proudly wear coveralls as we take measurements of the most up-to-date scientific instruments in deep water drilling operations. We are the men and women of the energy industry.

You can find us on the drill floor laughing and sometimes just getting on with things quietly and safely. You can see us in the yards in Aberdeen creating miles of tubular that will be plunged into a well by crews of drill crew deep into the dirt and seabed. You will hear us in the offices, having spent years offshore and now enjoying a more warm but often high-pressure time in the cosy chairs of executive-level management. You will see us in the rooms and corridors of platforms, ensuring your beds are clean and ready for you and putting your meals together to help you after that long shift outside on deck. You will hear us whistling as we aid the crane op on the jack-up and land his container of drill bits onto the vessel landing area, ready for backloading to Peterhead. We are the ones who throw ourselves into the industry across the world to not only provide us with a half-decent life of money and time off, but you will see our efforts to supply a way of life everyone enjoys.

I've had a long time to think about why we worked so well together and were able to see each other through callous times with smiles and sometimes a few tears. The reason why?

"We shared a connection."

We had this way of working out the kinks and connecting to and for one another. Did this mean we saw eye to eye in everything? Of course not; sometimes we fell out and felt I was talking to aliens from Mars, but always the connection was right, and the respect given. Between a few smokes in the tea shack or clanging irons together on the drill floor, wellheads, or the gym, we had this way of making the connection. Big scruffy, warm, caring men covered in sweat and tired to the bone after weeks of hard labour and having to learn many skills and create solutions to physical, mathematical, and, without a doubt, emotional issues that needed a fast-paced culture of closing the gap of failure to success. We had to find a way to make the connection. The drill pipe connection or attaching the bridge between the rig and the barge again after a storm forced it apart. I threw in the drill pipe from 90ft at the monkey board level and heard that latching smash as the drill pipe hit the back of the elevators. The driller picked up on his blocks, elevating the string so the roughnecks below could tail in the stand of 90ft iron drill pipe, apply the dope to the threads and ensure each spectacular rung of carved inch metal was spun in and torqued up to the correct psi for the specific grade of connection. We made the connection accurately and efficiently each time we ran this movement.

Sometimes, we had to carry out cement jobs, and there would be so many connections between the drill floor, pump room, and cement unit, all working together as a single organism to achieve a shared outcome. A cluster of men and women from many cultures and customs, all coming together to work on a shared result. The path to success offshore is knowing your outcome, planning with experience and data, acting, understanding what affects you're achieving, and with a sense of purpose, being willing to remain flexible until you succeed. No one makes it alone; it will always be a shared experience. It's more than teamwork. It's family.

EMBRACING OPEN HEARTEDNESS IN A WORLD OF CHALLENGES

"Deserves it! I daresay he does. Many that live deserve death. And some that die deserve life. Can you give it to them? Then do not be too eager to deal out death in judgement. For even the very wise cannot see all ends."
— J.R.R. Tolkien, The Fellowship of the Ring

Stress, anxiety, and burnout have become all too familiar in today's world. We often find ourselves amidst individuals who seem to lack empathy, disrupt conversations, project fake core values, and weave intricate webs of deception. These situations can be infuriating, leaving us to ponder whether people genuinely give their best or if that notion has become a far-fetched ideal, we've let go of.

Amidst this chaos, it's easy to overlook the immense power of our most profound resource - the human heart. Within its chambers lie our deepest emotions, the foundation of our values, and the wellspring of our ability for empathy and compassion.

Imagine if we stopped concerning ourselves with those empathy-lacking individuals. What if we ceased censoring our true selves to accommodate their comfort? What if we chose to live unguardedly, with an open heart? Far too often, we meet people with attitudes as foul as lingering farts, individuals who believe they dictate how others should feel because they prioritise their position over the wellbeing of their colleagues.

Living with an open-heart means embracing your life with vulnerability and authenticity. It means shedding fear and judgment and embracing the elegance of your imperfections. Through an open heart, we allow ourselves to be fully seen and heard and invite others to do the same.

The strength of an open heart lies in its potential to transform our personal lives and our shared human journey. We inspire others to follow suit when we present ourselves to the world with an open heart. We initiate a ripple effect of kindness, compassion, and understanding that can profoundly influence our communities, societies, and, ultimately, the world.

In a world that often exalts strength over vulnerability and emphasises individualism at the expense of community, nurturing open heartedness may appear daunting. It needs courage, stepping out of our comfort zones, and embracing the uncharted. However, in doing so, we unearth a realm of boundless possibilities, where hope isn't fleeting but a deep reservoir that sustains us through adversity.

Let us rise above those who lack empathy, transcending their influence. Let us acknowledge our wounds, seek help, and open ourselves to growth and connection. As we navigate the intricacies of our modern reality, let's remember the boundless power of the human heart. Let's expose ourselves to growth, connection, and transformation potential.

It is solely through open heartedness that we can genuinely unlock human progress. It's a superpower within us all, waiting to be embraced and with some effort, it could make things better.

Burnout: Understanding the Cumulative Effect of Stress

Burnout, often misconceived as the result of a single stressful event, is a slow accumulation of stress over an extended period. The duration of this build up directly changes the intensity and duration of the burnout itself, as well as the time it takes to recover fully.

It's essential to recognise that while work can contribute significantly to burnout, it's not always the sole cause. Stressors from various aspects of your life collectively contribute to this state. However, we emphasise work-related burnout in this book because a substantial part, about 70% or more, of our lives is at our workplaces.

Spotting burnout isn't overly complex either; there are several common indicators: persistent fatigue, emotional detachment, cynicism, pessimism, and a reduced ability to concentrate.

Around four years ago, the World Health Organization (WHO) transformed our feeling of burnout by officially categorising it as a medical diagnosis. It's no longer just a figure of speech; burnout is "a syndrome resulting from chronic workplace stress that has not been successfully managed."

The three primary symptoms outlined by the WHO include: Feelings of Energy Depletion or Exhaustion. Increased Mental Distance from One's Job or Negative Feelings. Reduced Professional Effectiveness.

For most of us, there are occasions at our jobs when we feel stressed, and we can manage it. A stressful week of work should be rewarded with relaxation at home, which helps reduce stress. However, what happens when this relief doesn't come?

A sense of depletion occurs when the pressure stays constant, and the stress doesn't dissipate. You start feeling disconnected and emotionally drained, even when you're away from work. The desire to mentally check out grows, but responsibilities and obligations hold you back. Often, the point where seeking help becomes imperative.

Both personal efforts and support from managers and superiors play a role in managing burnout. Creating a safe space to open up about your challenges and emotions isn't a sign of weakness; it's an act of tremendous courage. By doing so, not only do you give those around you insight into your situation, but their compassionate understanding also gives an opportunity for you and your colleagues to grow stronger, forge closer bonds, and become more effective as a team.

Overcoming ego is a pivotal step toward progress. When we collectively move beyond our concerns, we propel ourselves further than we could alone.

MENTAL HEALTH IN ENERGY

"It takes a great deal of bravery to stand up to our enemies, but just as much to stand up to our friends."
— J.K. Rowling, Harry Potter and the Sorcerer's Stone

Female Voices from Within

I have worked in HR for over 25 years and have always worked in the oil and gas industry. Thankfully, during my time as an HR Manager in the Industry, attitudes towards mental health have changed. However, a gendered stigma still exists that men should be stoic, strong and unemotional despite being away from home in harsh environments for weeks and missing the most critical times in their family's lives.

When I started my career in HR, mental health was not openly discussed. You were seen to be weak if you suffered any mental health illness, never mind talking about it!

In one incident I recall, a Senior Manager asked me into a meeting and said, " Did you know that this new employee in his team was on anti-depressants? I said I was unaware, but what difference would it make if he was? The answer I got astonished me; he said if I had known that I wouldn't have hired him. I answered so, if you had a person with diabetes and they had to take insulin, would you not hire them either? He said he will always be off ill, won't handle the pressure and stress, and certainly won't cope with being offshore, and I don't have time to deal with someone like that! – No wonder employees didn't want to speak up! Over the last 25 years, I have worked hard to try and change that stigma and was determined to get employees in the oil and gas industry to open up about and talk about mental health.

I remember another occasion, just a few years back, when I noticed over a few months that a very well-respected leader wasn't his usual optimistic self; he seemed withdrawn and was hiding away in his office. One night, there was just me and him in the building, and I went into his office, shut the door and said are you okay? You don't seem yourself. I got the usual "Yes, just busy." I pulled my chair up and said but are you really, okay? You can speak to me about anything; it won't go any further. He took a deep breath, and it all came out; I watched this seemingly strong man crumble in front of me, crying, telling me how he was failing at everything, working long hours, which was having a detrimental effect on his home life, and his health, he was suffering palpitations and was worried it was his heart, how it was all becoming too much for him. I let him talk, get it all out, and finally told him that nothing is more important than his health and family. You need to take time out and spend time with your family and focus on yourself; no job is worth making yourself ill for and get an appointment with your GP and get your heart checked.

A few months later, he phoned me to thank me, and he had moved on to a new role, which allowed him more time at home and was much happier; he had been to his GP, and his heart palpitations were purely stress.

So, what can companies do to get over the stigma of talking about mental health:

Promoting open conversations about mental health is vital for fostering a supportive work environment and encouraging men to express their feelings without fear of judgment. Workshops, seminars and awareness campaigns can normalise these conversations, highlighting that seeking help is a sign of strength, not weakness. Provide mental health resources and have Employee Assistance Programmes and counselling services readily available and promoted.

Leaders must lead by example, show vulnerability, share personal experiences with mental health challenges, and create a safe space for men to open up.

Train Managers and colleagues to recognise the signs of mental health struggles. We recently trained mental health first aiders; by providing that training, organisations can intervene early and offer the necessary support.

In conclusion, it is essential to acknowledge that everyone will likely encounter some form of mental health challenge at some point in their lives, whether it be grief, workplace stress, anxiety or depression. It is a shared human experience to face adversity, and organisations are responsible for extending their support. Progress has been made since the start of my HR journey. However, there is still a considerable journey ahead in destigmatising mental health discussions and ensuring employees feel comfortable acknowledging that it is acceptable not to be okay.

Shirley Butcher (FCIPD)

HR Manager

MAKING THE CONNECTION

Continued:

Fast forward almost a decade, and I have served on various crews and teams, and what they all knew about me and what I was deeply passionate about was the well-being and health of everyone I worked with. At home, I was well known for raising awareness of large-scale mental health campaigns within the armed forces, prisons, schools, universities, and the financial and construction Industry. During a hitch offshore with my scouse driller, he was taking care of business safely when he'd just drilled a section of the well and needed to carry out his actions to remove the top drive off the top of the drill pipe. As always, he let me know to "Open the Bleed Off", and I made my way to the standpipe manifold and started to crank open the valve, which was full of pressure from the rig pumps down in the pump room, which generated the needed force to pump the drilling mud and chemicals down the well through the entire fluid system much like the heart pumps blood through the body and nervous system.

Each drilling connection needs someone to release the built-up pressure via the bleed-off valve, which must occur every time. One of my passions is recognising how one system in life can make the connection and be of value in a foreign industry. This way of thinking was a strange trait. Still, I learned from an intelligent man called Jay Abraham, a marketing genius many years ago, that you must get everything you can from everything you've got.

That day, when I opened the bleed-off, I began to see how pressure and stress can be actively released in a safe environment, even surrounded by noise, ego, various voices, stubborn attitudes, and people who were not ready to see things as they could be. Macho culture is challenging and can often lead you down a dead-end regarding sensitive and complex areas such as well-being and mental health. Still, I felt I saw something that day, which was a feeling I had. I told Scouse about this as he always supported my mental health work, and he said, "Stevie, that makes perfect sense, " which is excellent coming from someone you like, trust, and care about. But also, bright and can see the potential.

It was a definitive moment where I began to make the connection of how I could actively help many more people in my Industry reduce stress levels and anxiety, which had been building up over the years. Or, at the very least, I could speak to them about my struggles and show them it's safe to be open and caring. Stigma isn't winning every battle!

It's no secret anymore just how serious mental health in the energy industry has become. I don't need to bore you with facts, but to refresh your memory, since I first started speaking out and stripping the stigma from mental health in 2007/8, I have watched the oil and gas and energy industry reach explosive levels of mental health and causing depression to increased, anxiety and stress levels have skyrocketed, burnouts continuing to grow each year. And more recently, men's average weight has increased, which can add to stress. It wasn't until 2018 that I began to share my concerns about the level of increased pressure and mental health-related issues I was learning about in our Industry and feeling myself.

I started to speak to the press and media. I created short documentaries highlighting issues such as depression and that it's not a weakness to experience these, especially as men, but something we all can suffer from if ignored and left to gather more pressure. The connection between higher stress at work and burnout was clear to me. When I spoke out, people's responses to my words included praise, gratitude, messages from lads offshore asking for my support, and questions from industry leaders about how to speak to their staff and teams. I was laughed at and mocked while on the rig. Change is challenging for some people and can be awkward and met by people's resistance, which is not an ego issue. It's more of an insecurity and tends to smooth out over time. Nothing deterred me, though. I knew my heart was focused, and I had to stand up for my beliefs, even when being laughed at or joked about behind my back. My desire to make a difference was tangible. I had started a connection, and I could feel what I had learned in the past decade was real-life experience and worthy of sharing. Instead of running full steam ahead like the young me, I thought about approaching this idea. Of how to share with people the concept of "Open the bleed off", I began searching for the best leaders in the game who came before me—strong people who have carved out their paths and understood the industry better than my 12 years. I was still working in the drilling industry, and mental health was still new to being discussed in the energy arena, so I had to play it smart. I decided to do the same thing I once did for the military and other industries nationwide.

I shared my stories and strategies to help organisations reach their teams. I knew I had to be willing to once again stand up for what I knew was correct and to carry this torch into the field as I had done many years prior. It was not an easy time for me. Supervisors ordered me to carry out tasks offshore amongst new people I had never worked with, which put my safety and health at significant risk. After being treated with disrespect for my voice of well-being, I decided I needed to take some time away from the operations. Instead of thinking I had taken a step back due to my increased blood pressure and work-related stress, I used every resource, from Employee Assistance Programmes to doctors and medical experts. I even sought the help of online counselling sessions, where I saw a chance to open the bleed-off for myself and speak out about my feelings. Work and the pressures of reduced staff and lower wages have hit everyone hard since the 2018 downturn. With redundancies hitting everyone from the rig to the office and beyond, it was clear something was close to boiling point. Not only with myself but with the industry and the thousands of people working to make a living but secretly hiding an unspoken system of rising pressures without any bleed-offs available. What would happen and has continued to happen was the beginning of many painful experiences at work and home.

It would be years later I found myself here! Away from the drill floor after the pandemic and redundancies decimated our Industry and way of life worldwide. They left tens of thousands out of work and needed help figuring out which way to look. The low oil prices of the 2018 slump were not healed, and we once again found ourselves hitting the hardest of times. Stress, fatigue, depression and anxiety all began to increase at a rate I was never ready to help with, and no matter how much help I focused on delivering, I couldn't keep up with demand.

This article is the foundation idea of a book I intend to write next year called "Open the Bleed Off" and will lay the truth of what I now see in real-time. I am about to share a snippet of what I am learning from hands-on experience earned the good old-fashioned way of working alongside the very men and women I care about. People face challenging times at work and home who have yet to have someone reach out to them and share the most significant opportunity of their time.

Mental health and well-being are the fabric of what will exponentially increase our people's potential. They will help increase bottom-line revenue over the years, keeping more good people in jobs and less of our teams off work due to burnout, fatigue, depression, anxiety and worse. Open the bleed-off is not simply a system; it's a living, breathing, working model that is active as we speak and even as I write.

Achieving successful results at the micro-level and with your help and open mind will help pioneer the macro as well. I can't do this alone and don't wish to either. Collaboration is always more fun and much better for everyone than competition. However, I am fiercely devoted to the well-being of everyone in our Industry, even those who may have a negative view of me; I wish you well, too. I am not in this business to be liked by you or the people I help; I am in this to inspire and pioneer the game I love—the game of life, business and well-being at all levels.

In short, the definitive results reach out not only from our Industry but also helping hundreds of other struggling economies find a much greater level of health. After all, as I said to Energy Voice in August 2019

"We need to remember – it's staring everyone in the face – it's not safety and health, it's health and safety. "Health is the keyword, and it's at the very beginning."

The truth of my mental health journey has been shared many times across the media, but what I am so profoundly obsessed with isn't my story but the underlying stories across the many teams and families that I am working with from oil and gas, military, teenagers, prisoners and prison officers, construction workers and the list goes on until you are left feeling a sense of growing pain and trauma that is being approached with a lack of understanding and without respect for what is needed. We are not broken and will not snap if you try and talk to us. People need to be heard at their level first to feel understood and allowed to open the bleed-off on their stories, just as I have. Others have, and I can tell you with deep conviction and truth every time someone has spoken to me and opened up about their stress and pain, the levels in their pressured system instantly begin to lower back down to a much safer and far healthier space, just like when I was on the drill floor and opened the bleed off to release the pressure built up on the drilling system via the valve on the standpipe manifold.

We, too, can open the valves and release the systems we hold all this pressure from built-up anxiety and stress, which gather more force until the day comes. We've all been guilty of this when you either explode and lose your temper, quit, say the wrong thing or do bad things. I know I have. Or you implode. And we can all place our hands on our hearts and express deep pain for someone who has gone down this road. It is the elephant in the room, and no one wants to speak about it, but there it lies. Suicide, the end of the line, and the implosion of all the pressure stacked up over months and years of not opening the bleed-offs and not speaking to someone eventually lead us to the painful path of "it's all too much" and we can't find a way out. Hence, we let it build to dangerous levels that are toxic to our minds, bodies, teams, and staff.

Just like the pressurised systems on the drill floor can be ignored or pushed to the limit of dangerous levels of stress or a system of connections like a cement job can cause failures or fractures in the design of the drill string and well integrity or in a chemical plant, a dairy factory or a team of athletes, or your family. Suppose we do not take the time to give one another the space to "open up and open out" to bleed off the pressure that has become too hard to deal with. In that case, it is stored and stays dormant like a small volcano.

It's a simple analogy, but it makes perfect sense. A child can understand it, has the potential to help alleviate stress, and provides excellent resources to your team and valued members across your organisation. I know this for sure as I have been privileged to consult and speak for many years now the organisations across the UK that serve the oil and gas industry, including Bilfinger Salamis, who asked me to provide a full day of speaking and conversations where I spoke with a very open manner and spent the day with both management, operations teams in the offices and also their yard staff where I gave three speeches in one day to ensure their crews working down the yard got to hear my story on why mental health and wellness isn't simply about awareness campaigns. Still, instead, it's the fabric of what makes us happy and healthy and supplies the core values of what we all treasure—a happy life.

Or when I delivered training workshops and talked to the trauma teams at RGU alongside the great and late Professor David Alexander. I shared my ideas and lessons learned in battle and the North Sea. I worked alongside the spectacular Susan Klein, who was at the time Director of Aberdeen Centre for Trauma Research, and we worked alongside her students and teams. I've since been sharing my stories and experiences with an inspiring company. I developed the final piece to my "Making the Connection." it was after being asked by a senior HR member from

Tenaris in Aberdeen to come and give a heartfelt speech and offer some insight into mental health and wellness.

Right from the start, I knew this was not a poster campaign or a glossy lip service filler—a change of perspective after a trauma occurred within the workers was needed. Sadly, the staff and teams of Tenaris had experienced a profound loss and had come to me for some genuine help in this matter. They needed someone to reach their working teams at the yard and speak to them about depression, anxiety and, most importantly, suicide. Having been in this position for many years, I was honoured to help and asked if we could carry out this day with some real, honest, heart-to-heart conversations. I felt it was time to share my idea of opening the bleed-off. Tenaris' senior HR management team was thrilled to listen, and after discussion, the day went ahead.

I had no poster, notes, glossy folders, or notepads. I had no gifts to hand out and no PowerPoint slides to show. I had only one moment to speak to these men and reach them where it mattered- the core of any great individual or team- the heart.

I used this engagement session to speak the truth and to invite them into the safest space where they felt empowered enough to put down their phones and cups of tea and give me their full attention. I wasn't trying to impose my theories or awareness of some idea; I was using the power of my past and my honest story of how I'd come to learn the truth about mental health. When my talk ended, I invited them to ask me anything in a Q&A style session that was quick and easy for a rapid result. They began to open up about not only their struggles with everyday pressures but also that they have been holding in some things and felt for the first time they could safely vent off and feel it was okay to do it. They began to open after hearing me speak to them about my vulnerabilities and moments of genuine hurt, stress, and anxiety over the years from everyday life pressures. The speaking was healing in a real-time environment. Just like releasing the stored energy on the drill floor using the bleed-off valve, speaking to the teams and management, they all expressed a sense of lowered stress and increased confidence to reach out and ask the tough questions they had been holding on for too long. They felt this was one of the most engaging sessions they had ever taken part in. I was intensely proud of Tenaris and the men for having the pioneering spirit to hold this day and to help move the conversation forward in mental health. Things were only getting started. I didn't even get out of the building, and the lads asked to speak to me outside while they were having a tea break; I said yeah, of course, and followed them out. There were around three lads, and they all said they wanted to know when I was coming back and if it would be okay to reach out to me and have a one-to-one conversation about their concerns and hopes for their health. I was inspired emotionally and so proud of their courage, and of course, we did.

Tenaris reached out again and asked if we could continue to grow this clear and empowering relationship the teams had begun to see simply by speaking out with me and having me listen and offer my real-life experiences. I was invited back to Tenaris a second time to speak and present a half-day session where I entered the teams working on site. Management kindly offered a guided tour from the operations leader, who helped me reach the men working in their everyday positions; it allowed us all to open up to one another and share our connections from working in the same Industry. As the manager and I walked around moving through each department and taking a reasonable length of time to speak to individuals one-on-one and as a group during working hours and without having to halt the operations, it was a genuinely enriching gift. I also had the chance to discuss some critical moments with the manager himself. He spoke about some of his genuine care for his team and crews; often, the most demanding roads are from the highest positions, and I, too, could feel how deeply he cared for his workforce.

After the main speech and Q&A, then the walk around and talks, I was asked to come back a third time, where the crew and I had a chance to talk one-on-one while they took breaks from their work under no pressure or obligation. They came in one by one and sat with me in total confidence. We spoke openly and with genuine hearts about their feelings about tension from home life, kids, girlfriends, work-life balance, and the truth of their worry about depression and recent suicides that had shaken them. We spoke without stress and discussed everything they needed to get off their chest. And it worked. The valve was being turned even for a small moment. I could feel these men sitting within their vulnerability, and it was such a wonderful moment for me as the person they chose to open up to. I could see a genuine moment of humanity happening. The men told me they felt better for having spoken with me. If you have ever been in this feeling yourself after someone shares their truths with you or concerns and they have a greater focus, relaxed posture, and seem to stand tall, you know it's an excellent place for anyone to be, especially at work and around the office or yard. When the stress is released, you are in more significant health, and its increased safety and is the best feeling of being well. Wellbeing is the key.

The session was so helpful and worked so quickly. Again, I was invited to Tenaris a third time, which proved my work was having an impact. My job was having a great result, so Tenaris executives asked me to provide more coaching with my compassionate level of speech, Q&A and conversations with their international teams working abroad. Others were in quarantine due to arriving at their site in various locations around the globe. At first, the lads I had on the team's call via my office at home (my kitchen) were a bit shy to have their cameras on and opted for audio-only. That's fair, I thought, as I'm a total stranger. I began to share my story as I had done many times, and slowly but surely, the cameras turned on. I could see their faces and reactions, but mostly, I could feel their trust in me grow, and the responses were beautiful. They had begun to make the connection with me. They shared confidence in one another, started speaking to me, and had great conversations. It was truly remarkable to listen and be of value to Tenaris teams as they were away from home, in hotels, and on the rigs as they prepared to go to work. Men speak about sensitive issues such as depression, anxiety, time away from loved ones, COVID-19, etc.

What I have come to learn, in all my years since I started back when I was 26 and now 43, is speaking out for wellbeing and mental health. It's not simply a one-way awareness campaign. It's not a poster or a new string of words we use to highlight our way of seeing things. There is nothing new about mental health we don't already have a concern about: depression, burnout, anxiety, suicide.

What I have uncovered during my work over the last few years from having my mind, heart, and imagination open is the answers are within our ability to speak to one another without the added pressure of having to carry out another course or spend even more time away from loved ones, or without having to cast nets out to see if anyone will come and use the EAP that is nice. Still, it must reduce the rising cases hitting our most cherished teams. Wouldn't you prefer to have a conversation that not only was it safer at the work site, but you didn't have to utilise the EAP, which is, after the fact, much more powerful to lead than to feel it's too late?

Mental health is the single most important conversation of our time. When we speak from the heart, we reach the hearts of others. If we ask people to tick another box, we can only expect to get a little in the way back of honest, heartfelt feedback. So, what is this about?

Vulnerability, Openness, Humility, Empathy.

These are the key ingredients I have shared with you in this chapter. I have tried to avoid boring you with facts, and I've not plastered across the bullet points I intended to make. I have shared from my heart in the hope I can reach yours. Having worked with Tenaris and being gratefully shown around their incredible site the past few weeks and since working with them in October 2020, I have come to learn something.

All those years working on the drill floor and pipe decks, preparing and running in miles and miles of tubulars for completion packages that would enable us to produce the oil and gas we drilled for. The most essential part of every task was ensuring the connections were true, held integrity, and were sent into the darkness with all the confidence we could muster. I had the privilege to witness the precise and top-rated connections I've spent years running on the drill floors crafted and created before me. I watched them being turned, milled, shaped, and prepared with focused effort, safety, and a sense of pride above all. I felt the connection coming full circle that day a few weeks ago. In 2009, when Scouse was teaching me about drilling and the art of the drill floor, working pressures, stress on the system, and why we have to "open the bleed off", gave me an insight I would later use in the way I communicate and help in the most straightforward manner possible to the thousands of individuals, teams, organisations, and industries so they not only can show their staff how much they care but this, in turn, helped me see with profound clarity how our Industry could provide the framework and network for how mental health is spoken about in the years to come.

We all have the power to "Open the bleed-off" in our teams and places of work. We supply the real-time and real-life ability to make and share the connections that lead us and our loved ones into a healthier future. With a bit of work and some heart, we can help those struggling to reach out and give them the story that might be the catalyst they need to open the valves of their mind and heart that leads to the happiest years of their working life.

I know you care, so contact my organisation and me via LinkedIn to help you bring this service to the heart of your business. Your people! And let's create some truly inspired moments where your people finally learn to open the bleed-off in their own lives and make that connection for themselves.

THE UNSPOKEN METHOD

ASK, HELP, HOPE, HEAL

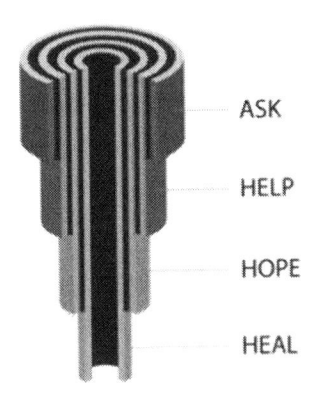

THE UNSPOKEN METHOD - THE AHHH MODEL
ASK, HELP, HOPE, HEAL

The Power of Asking for Help

In the depths of our struggles and the weight of our burdens, there exists a transformative force, a catalyst that can set us free from the chains of stress and burnout. Asking for help is a force so simple yet so profound.

In this chapter, we embark on a journey to unlock the immense power of this small act, for within it lies the key to opening the bleed-off and finding healing and hope.

In the vast tapestry of life, we all meet big and small challenges. Often, we try to shoulder the weight of the world alone, believing that seeking help is a sign of weakness or vulnerability. But let me assure you, it is quite the opposite. Asking for help is an act of strength, courage, and self-compassion.

As we delve into the four pillars of the unspoken method—Ask, Help, Hope, Heal—we will discover how each step is intertwined, forming a robust framework for personal growth and transformation. Today, we shine a light on the first pillar: The Power of Asking for Help.

Asking for help is not just a request for aid; it is an acknowledgement that we are human and can't afford to believe we must navigate this journey alone. It is an act of vulnerability, a profound willingness to open our hearts and minds to the support and understanding of others. It may seem daunting, but it is in asking for help that we unlock a wellspring of compassion for ourselves and those around us.

In a world that often glorifies self-reliance, we must recognise the immense strength in reaching out for support. The act of asking for help is a bridge that connects us, fostering deeper connections and genuine human relationships. When we embrace vulnerability, we create a safe space for others to do the same, cultivating a community of empathy and understanding.

Throughout these pages, we will meet stories of resilience, courage, and transformation—stories of individuals who dared to ask for help and experienced profound growth. These stories will serve as beacons of hope, reminding us that we are never alone on this journey.

So, I invite you to embrace the power of asking for help. As you read this chapter and beyond, I encourage you to reflect on your life and the areas where you may be carrying the world's weight in silence. Let us open the bleed-off together, release the pressure, and step into a new chapter of healing and hope. Remember, in asking for help, we unlock the door to a more vibrant and empowered life. Let the journey begin.

ASK – The first step in the unspoken method

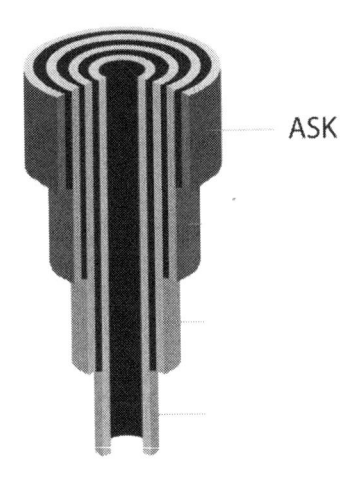

Ask for Help: Even the most independent individuals need help sometimes. When facing a challenging situation, don't hesitate to ask for help. It's a sign of courage and openness, not weakness.

In the realm of industry, stress permeates the very fabric of existence. It wraps its invisible tendrils around the souls of those who dare to venture into the realm of energy, oil, gas, and renewables. It is an unrelenting force that knows no boundaries, infiltrating every corner of our being.

Stress looms large like an ominous cloud in the vast expanse of the oil and gas sector. The pressure to extract, explore, and meet insatiable demands weighs heavy on those who toil in its depths. The relentless pursuit of progress and the ever-present spectre of environmental concerns create tension that seeps into every fibre of their being. It is a constant battle between the drive for profit and the weight of responsibility, leaving them teetering on exhaustion.

But even in renewable energy, stress finds its way, sneaking through the cracks of noble intentions. The urgency to combat climate change and the relentless push for innovation, places an immense burden on those at the forefront of the revolution. The weight of saving the planet rests upon their shoulders as they strive to find sustainable solutions amidst a world hungry for change. The stakes are high, and the pressure can be suffocating.

In the darkest corners of our hearts and minds, a silent struggle often brews, hidden from the world behind a facade of strength. We carry the weight of the world, feeling the burden of stress and burnout, believing that asking for help would be a sign of weakness or inadequacy. Yet, dear reader, precisely in those moments of vulnerability, we find the unyielding power of asking for help.

Allow me to share a personal story that etched the importance of seeking help into the very fibre of my being. While in the army, I embarked on a life-changing tour in Iraq. The scorching heat bore down upon us, unyielding like the pressure that often consumes us daily. One fateful day, the relentless sun bared its teeth into my body, and I felt the grip of heatstroke tightening around my throat.

As I stumbled and faltered under the searing sun, I realised that if I didn't get fluids and salts into my system, I could collapse, made ineffective in the face of imminent danger. The enemy fire rained upon us, leaving no room for hesitation or doubt. I knew I had to act fast, and in that moment of profound vulnerability, I turned to my fellow soldiers for help.

With the weight of my life hanging in the balance, I mustered the courage to call out to my mates, uttering those three words that would forever alter my perspective: "I need help."

In that simple yet profound request for aid, I laid bare the struggles I had been silently carrying. My foolish pride and fears about what people would think of me dissolved in the face of necessity. I recognised that strength lies not in enduring hardship alone but in having the courage to reach out when our burdens become too heavy.

The collective response from my mates was swift and unwavering. In camaraderie and solidarity, they rallied around me, offering their support and ensuring I received the needed aid. In that moment of vulnerability, I truly understood the power of asking for help.

Our lives are not a battlefield, but we will face trials and challenges that can leave us overwhelmed and alone. We may grapple with stress, burnout, or emotional turmoil, unwilling to show our vulnerability to the world. But in those moments of challenge, we must dare to break free from the chains of secrecy and reach out for support.

Asking for help is not an admission of weakness but an acknowledgement of our shared humanity. It is an act of courage and strength, a declaration that we deserve more than to bear the world's weight alone. Just as I found solace in the arms of my comrades during that harrowing moment in Iraq, you, too, can find support and understanding in the arms of those who care about you.

In life's journey, we must remember that vulnerability is not a sign of defeat but a testament to our courage. And in asking for help, we discover the resilience of the human spirit—the power to overcome adversity and rise above the darkness that threatens to consume us.

So, when the world's weight presses upon your shoulders and the stress threatens to engulf you, remember that asking for help is not a sign of weakness but a beacon of strength. Embrace the unyielding power of vulnerability, for it is in the openness of our hearts that we find healing, hope, and the unwavering support of those who stand beside us.

The Unyielding Power of Asking for Help

In the labyrinth of life, we often find ourselves navigating treacherous terrains alone, believing that our independence is the key to survival. We tread carefully, fearing that asking for help might cast a shadow of weakness upon us. But dear reader, I implore you to consider this: Asking for help is not a testament to vulnerability but a beacon of courage and strength.

In the tapestry of your story, when you feel under the dark clouds of hurt, pain and frustration, you can be stitched together by threads of compassion and empathy. At some point, each of us will meet challenges that test the limits of our endurance. And in those moments of trial, seeking help is not a sign of frailty; instead, it is an acknowledgement of our shared humanity.

Just as the mightiest oak stands tall and proud, it, too, must draw sustenance from the earth and gather strength from its roots. So, too, must we lean upon the support of others to weather the storms that life bestows upon us. Asking for help is not an admission of defeat but a proclamation of bravery—a declaration that we are willing to be vulnerable and trust in the kindness of those around us.

As independent souls, we might be hesitant to unburden ourselves, believing that our struggles should remain concealed from the world. But precisely in those moments of openness, we find the unyielding power of connection. When we dare to share our challenges, we create a bridge between hearts—a pathway for understanding and empathy to flow freely.

Think back to when you extended a helping hand to someone in need. Did you perceive this person as weak? Or did you see their courage in reaching out for help? As you embrace their vulnerability with compassion, so will others embrace yours.

Life is an intricate dance of highs and lows, joys and sorrows, victories and defeats. And amid this symphony, we are gifted with the presence of others who walk beside us. Our friends, family, and loved ones are not merely spectators in the grand theatre of our lives; they are willing participants, ready to lend a hand when the music grows overwhelming.

When the world's weight presses upon your shoulders, do not be afraid to seek solace in the arms of others. In asking for help, we discover the true strength of our connections—the resilience and power that lies within the embrace of a caring community.

I invite you to embrace the courage within you, to unfurl the wings of vulnerability and soar on the currents of trust. Together, we will navigate the stormy seas of life, weathering the challenges and celebrating the triumphs, for it is in asking for help that we find unity and healing—a powerful reminder that we are never truly alone in this journey.

Unearthing the Fear of Asking for Help

In the vast canvas of life, fear is a formidable adversary lurking in the shadows, whispering doubts and insecurities into our minds. The fear of asking for help looms large among its many masks, shrouding us in a cloak of hesitancy and self-doubt. It is an invisible barrier that holds us back from seeking the support we need, convincing us that to ask is to display weakness or burden others.

Yet, within this apprehension lies a pivotal truth that we must confront with unwavering resolve. The fear of asking for help does not show inadequacy; it is a shared human experience that transcends boundaries and embraces us all. To overcome this fear is to embrace our humanity—to acknowledge that every one of us, no matter our station in life, will at times require the guiding hand of another.

When we grapple with this trepidation, pausing and reflecting upon its origin is crucial. Often, it appears from the deeply ingrained belief that independence is the cornerstone of strength—to rely on others is to expose a vulnerability that can be manipulated or exploited. But this belief is a fallacy, a mirage that distorts the true essence of strength.

Consider for a moment the journey of a lone oak tree standing tall against the elements. Its branches may sway and bend, but its roots delve deep into the earth, intertwined with the origins of neighbouring trees. They fortify one another in unity, standing stronger against the storms threatening to uproot them. In this same way, human strength is not measured solely by individual fortitude but by our ability to connect, support, and uplift one another.

To overcome the fear of asking for help is to embark on a journey of self-empowerment—to recognise that your self-worth is not worthy of inclusion or development or, in fact, a weakness by seeking help, but rather enhanced by the bonds we forge in doing the work to improve yourself. The courage to ask is a triumph—a declaration that we are unafraid to embrace our imperfections and trust in the compassion of those around us.

In the dance of life, we must learn to extend a hand and receive it in kind. When we hold back from asking, we deny others the opportunity to expand their kindness, empathy, and love. In doing so, we deny ourselves the gift of connection—a skill that has the power to heal, transform, and uplift.

As we venture into the depths of this chapter, let us shatter the illusion of fear and embrace the truth that asking for help is to sow the seeds of growth and resilience. Together, we shall navigate the labyrinth of trepidation and emerge victorious, unshackled from the fear that once held us captive. In overcoming this fear, we unlock the boundless potential of our shared humanity. This potential flourishes in the tender embrace of support and understanding.

Unshackling the Fear of Asking for Help

In the bustling corridors of the oil and gas industry, where steel meets determination and ambition fuels progress, lies a cohort of unsung heroes—the men and women of HR.

Managers, Recruitment, QHSE, Training and the people who assist within the beating heart of this ever-evolving sector carry the responsibility of balancing the scales of compassion and efficiency, ensuring the well-being of their colleagues while navigating their own unique set of challenges.

Picture this—a bright morning at the oil and gas headquarters. Amongst the sea of stern faces and assertive voices, you'll find Alex, an HR manager with a vision of fostering a workplace that thrives on empathy, communication, and inclusivity. But beneath Alex's confident demeanour lies a story that mirrors the struggle of countless others in the industry.

One day, during a particularly challenging phase at work, Alex found himself juggling the complexities of a crucial employee appraisal.

Alex had been holding a lot in and taking the pressure home, causing friction with his girlfriend. He'd become slightly off with her and was not speaking about his stuff. The emotions and feelings about how the pressure was creeping up on him, and instead of opening to his partner, he buried it. Fear of looking weak and unmanly caused him to become less of a man. It's strange how the fear of asking for help limits us from being better versions of ourselves. Not only was Alex losing ground at work, but he would also lose his relationship over time, which would be devastating.

The pressure was immense, and the weight of responsibilities threatened to pull him under. Like many others, Alex was determined to prove himself in an environment often dominated by an old-fashioned, overly masculine culture.

But despite the bravado, a gnawing fear lurked in the shadows—the fear of asking for help. Admitting vulnerability was seen as a chink in the armour, a potential setback to progress. And so, Alex held on, pushing forward with a stoic resolve, even as the pressure grew and stress mounted.

Amid this turmoil, an unexpected encounter changed the course of events. It was a casual conversation with Sarah, a seasoned HR professional who had seen her share of ups and downs in the industry. Over a cup of coffee, Alex decided to confide in her, sharing the burden he carried, the fear that weighed upon his shoulders.

"You know, Sarah, I've been feeling overwhelmed lately. The appraisal process has me on edge, and I'm worried about falling short."

"I get it, Alex. It's a tough spot to be in. But remember, you don't have to carry this all alone. We're a team and here to support each other."

What happened next was nothing short of a revelation. Sarah listened without judgment or condescension. She offered not just sympathy but genuine understanding, revealing that she, too, had once grappled with the same fear. She shared how, by reaching out for help, she discovered the power of collective strength, of fostering an environment that embraced vulnerability and communication.

"When I was in your shoes a while back, I felt the same way—scared to ask for help, worried about seeming incompetent. But trust me, it's liberating when you realise that we all need support sometimes."

"But what if people think I can't handle the pressure? That I'm not cut out for this role?

"Listen, Alex, asking for help doesn't make you weak; it makes you human. And you're doing a damn good job here. We all have our moments, and that's okay. The key is to learn and grow from them."

In that moment, a spark ignited within Alex—a realisation that asking for help was not a sign of weakness but a gesture of courage and bravery. By breaking free from the constraints of self-sufficiency, he understood that he could create a workplace that thrived on shared humanity, where men and women in HR could feel empowered to support one another.

"Hey babe, that's me home, by the way. I've grabbed some of your favourite Chinese and a bottle of that red wine your mate said was on a deal at Tesco; it looks nice. I thought you deserved a little treat." Alex walked in the door of his flat, where his girlfriend was trying to unwind with their dog after a manic day.

"No way, that's so thoughtful. Aww, babe, thanks. What's brought this on?"

"Honestly, I'm sorry, I've been so distant these last few weeks, and I totally felt under pressure with work, and I just needed to remind you how important you are and that everything you do for me is noticed"

"Alex, why didn't you say something?"

"I was scared to admit I needed help, but today at work, I got chatting with Sarah. She reminded me how she was in my position once and that asking for help is a bold, courageous move we all need to make."

"Sarah sounds pretty smart."

"She is such a great boss. Instead of looking down on me, she taught me something valuable."

"Yeah, what's that then?"

"Asking for help is the opposite of weakness, and yeah, I've been a twat at home the last week."

"Open the wine, you big twat"

As he poured the wine, Alex felt the pressure of the last few weeks release. He saw a smile on his partner's face, which made him smile, and he realised that holding onto all that stress and pressure is a waste of time. Asking for help leads to a deeper connection with loved ones, a chance to feel close to those we care about and, in his case, wine.

The story of Alex is not an isolated incident; it reflects a much broader truth. In an industry that demands resilience and perseverance, we must recognise that vulnerability does not weaken us; it strengthens us. By unshackling the fear of asking for help, we pave the way for a culture that celebrates the balance of masculine and feminine qualities that embraces empathy and collaboration.

As the men and women of HR, foster an environment where open communication and support are encouraged and celebrated. Let us champion the cause of inclusivity and understanding, knowing that our collective strength lies in our willingness to seek assistance to lean on one another when the weight becomes too much to bear alone.

Through these acts of courage, we break free from the confines of an old-fashioned, overly masculine culture and pave the way for an industry that embraces the true power of human connection. In doing so, we enrich our workplace with compassion, empathy, and growth, making it a space where everyone, regardless of gender, thrives and flourishes. So, the next time you feel the world's weight upon your shoulders, don't be afraid to say those three magic words: "I need help." It is through asking that we not only heal ourselves but create a powerful force of support that elevates us all.

Ask yourself these questions and see if you can reach a more open-minded way of thinking when asking for help.

- How can we foster a workplace culture where asking for help is encouraged and celebrated as a collaborative strength?

- Have you ever seen a colleague seek help and been inspired by their courage?

- How can we create an environment where everyone feels empowered to do the same?

- Are there any barriers preventing some employees from feeling comfortable asking for help? How can we break down these barriers together?

- What resources or support systems can we implement to ensure every team member can access the help they need to thrive in their roles?

- How can we promote the idea that asking for help doesn't mean weakness but rather a shared commitment to achieving our collective goals?

- Are there any specific situations where you struggled and wish you had asked for help sooner? How can we learn from these experiences to encourage proactive help-seeking?

- What strategies can we adopt to ensure that all team members feel equally comfortable seeking help and support regardless of their background or position?

- How can we incorporate regular check-ins and open conversations about people's challenges to create a more supportive and empathetic work environment?

- What can leaders and managers do to set an example and normalise asking for help as a part of personal and professional growth?

- How can we celebrate and acknowledge the instances where someone asks for help and its positive impact on the individual and team dynamic?

In this journey of understanding the Unspoken Method, we have delved into the transformative power of asking for help and the courage it takes to overcome our fears and seek support. We've learned that no matter how strong, independent, or capable we may be, there are moments when we all need a helping hand. It's not a sign of weakness but a testament to our shared humanity.

Asking for help is a gateway to deeper connections and mutual understanding. It allows us to express gratitude for the optimistic energy others bring into our lives. We build networks, foster relationships, and create support communities through this vulnerability.

But let's remember the profound impact that asking for help can have on our lives. When we open ourselves to help, we often discover unforeseen solutions, valuable resources, and connections that make a tremendous difference in navigating the challenges that come our way.

Of course, it can be challenging to ask for help. The fear of appearing inadequate or burdening others can hold us back. But here, we've come to understand that true strength lies in breaking through that fear. Embracing the idea that everyone needs help at times, regardless of position or background, empowers us to reach out with openness and courage.

In the HR world, where employees' well-being is at the forefront, understanding the importance of asking for help becomes even more critical. HR professionals play a vital role in fostering an environment where seeking support is accepted and encouraged. They can cultivate an inclusive and supportive atmosphere by leading by example and creating a workplace culture that values vulnerability and collaboration.

As we move forward into the realm of hope, let us understand that asking for help is a powerful tool for growth and resilience. It paves the way for hope to flourish, knowing that when we face challenges together, there is strength in unity.

In the next phase of the Unspoken Method, we will explore hope's transformative power and how it can be a beacon of light in the darkest times. We will learn that hope is not merely wishful thinking but a force that propels us forward, even when the odds seem insurmountable. We will uncover hope's untold potential in helping us heal and thrive.

PART THREE

LEADING TO PROMOTE MENTAL HEALTH

To handle yourself, use your head; to handle others, use your heart."
— Eleanor Roosevelt

Establishing Trust in Leadership

At the core of every successful organisation lies a foundation of trust in its leadership. Trust is the glue that binds teams together, fostering a sense of psychological safety and empowerment. When employees trust their leaders, they feel secure in sharing their challenges, seeking guidance, and embracing vulnerability.

Building trust within a workplace begins with transparent and open communication. Leaders must be authentic in their interactions, admitting their mistakes and vulnerabilities. By being honest about their journey and challenges, leaders prove that it is safe for others to do the same.

Consistency is vital to nurturing trust. Leaders must follow through on their promises and act with integrity. When employees see that their leaders lead by example, it fosters a culture of trustworthiness throughout the organisation.

Moreover, empowering employees to take ownership of their work and offering autonomy reinforces trust. When individuals feel that their ideas and contributions are valued, they become more invested in the organisation's success.

Creating a Tipping Point for Workplace Mental Health

To promote mental health in the workplace, we can make a tipping point—a moment when positive changes cascade throughout the organisation.

A critical aspect of this tipping point lies in the recognition and validation of mental health struggles. Acknowledging that mental health is an integral part of overall well-being helps destigmatise discussions about mental health challenges. When organisations prioritise mental health, it sends a powerful message to employees that their well-being is valued and supported.

Fostering a supportive ecosystem that encourages seeking help is pivotal in creating the tipping point. By supplying accessible resources, such as counselling services, mental health workshops, and support groups, organisations show their commitment to employee well-being. Additionally, making mental health a regular part of the workplace conversation through training and awareness programs reinforces the message that seeking help is not only accepted but encouraged.

Leaders must play a central role in championing this tipping point. By sharing their own experiences with mental health challenges and the support they received, leaders lead by example. Moreover, offering flexibility and understanding when employees need time for self-care creates an environment where mental health feels prioritised for the entire team.

Embracing Help: A Collective Journey

The Unspoken Method of seeking help is a collective journey involving individuals and leadership working together to create a culture of openness, empathy, and compassion. Organisations can build a solid foundation for promoting mental health by fostering authentic connections and showing trust.

Together, we can create workplaces where seeking help is seen as a strength, not a weakness. A workplace where individuals can bring their lives to work without feeling they can't be who they are. Free from fear of judgment, and where mental health is a priority, not an afterthought.

As leaders and team members, we can create a ripple effect, spreading the message that seeking help is not only acceptable but essential. By embracing the Unspoken Method and leading with purpose, we ignite a transformational shift in workplace mental health that resonates far beyond the confines of our organisations and into the fabric of society itself.

In the following chapters, we will delve deeper into the practical strategies and steps needed to make the Unspoken Method a living reality within our workplaces. Together, let us embark on this journey to create thriving, supportive, and compassionate environments where everyone can flourish and unlock their full potential.

HELP - THE SECOND STEP IN THE UNSPOKEN METHOD

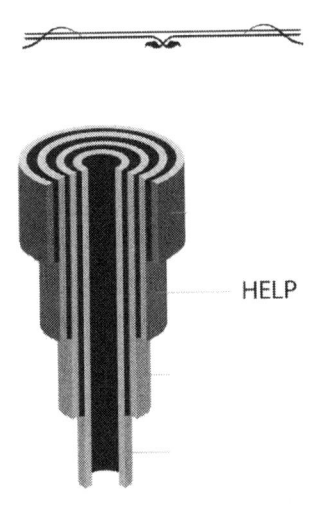

HELP

Can you help me? We all need to lean on each other from time to time. With this, we will keep the simplest human values—the need for connection. Helping not only unifies us and gives us strength, but it also reshapes the way we live our lives.

HELP - The Power of Unspoken Kindness

In the vastness of life, some threads bind us together, weaving a beautiful pattern of human connection. One of the most profound threads that run through our journey is the simple yet transformative act of HELP. In the unspoken method, we find that HELP is not just about aiding; it reflects our humanity and shared journey.

I need to be upfront with you; in doing so, I am completely open, vulnerable, and frank. I'll admit it—I suck at asking for help. It's ironic, I know. Here I am, writing a book about the power of seeking help, yet I struggle with it myself. Maybe this is my way of confronting my failings (I can almost hear my dad laughing at me). I suspect it stems from being rejected at birth by my biological father and growing up having to be very self-reliant. It's challenging to ask people to help me; it makes me feel weaker, and it's a battle I've been trying hard to overcome in recent years.

One area where I've been actively practising asking for help is within a group of copywriters, I'm part of. We work as a team, serving one of the fastest-growing coaching companies online. Every day, we log into Slack and download the spreadsheet on GDrive to see which clients need their sales pages, email sequences, lead magnets, and offers worked on. I love this work, and I'm compensated well for it. But deep down, I've found it hard to ask for help when I doubt my abilities. The dreaded imposter syndrome can be downright debilitating at times.

However, one thing I'm sure of is that I love writing and the work I do. So, with much courage, I decided to open up about my insecurities to my team. To my surprise, they embraced this side of me, showing me a level of open-minded growth and kindness, I'm not used to in the workplace. This newfound vulnerability hasn't just made me happier in my side hustle; it has also allowed me to flourish in my copywriting skills. I've grown as a writer and coach and become an in-house expert for hundreds of clients. Finding the courage to ask for help has been a game changer for me within my small entrepreneurial circle.

In this journey, I've noticed that my mentor, who runs a rapidly growing $2 million-a-year online digital marketing business, also excels at asking for help. She allows her team to take charge, and in doing so, she achieves remarkable results and outcomes. It's scary at first but embracing vulnerability and seeking help has allowed me to grow as a person within the culture she has created, and it inspires me to be better at my work.

Now, you might be wondering how my story can help you. Well, if you've read this far (thank you), you'll relate to those moments when life puts immense pressure on your shoulders. The family demands, bills, responsibilities, and work obligations are endless. And amidst it all, we often forget to ask for help. The fear of appearing weak keeps us from seeking the support we need.

But I've learned from my journey that true strength lies in vulnerability. Asking for help is not a sign of weakness; it shows our humanity and willingness to grow. So, let's embrace the courage to seek help when we need it most. In doing so, we may find that the barriers we once faced begin to crumble, and a world of possibilities opens before us.

Let me share with you a story from the unspoken method, a story that embodies the essence of HELP.

It was a chilly winter evening when a young woman named Maya found herself stranded at a bus stop. The night was dark, and the streets were quiet. Feeling a sense of unease, Maya clutched her coat tightly, hoping the bus would arrive soon.

As minutes turned into what felt like hours, Maya's anxiety grew. That's when an older woman named Henrietta approached her. With a warm smile and a gentle voice, the lady asked if she was alright and if she needed any help. Maya hesitated at first, but there was something in Henrietta's eyes that reassured her.

Henrietta shared her experience of being stranded at a bus stop in her youth and how a stranger's kindness had made all the difference. She offered to wait with Maya until the bus arrived, providing her with company and a sense of safety in the night.

As they sat together, Henrietta shared more stories from her life, imparting wisdom and encouragement to Maya. When the bus finally arrived, she felt grateful for the ride and the unexpected connection she had made that night. Henrietta's HELP had turned a moment of fear into warmth and compassion.

This story from the unspoken method reminds us that HELP is not just about grand gestures or elaborate displays of charity. Found in the simplest acts, the ones that happen in everyday moments. A kind word, a listening ear, a helping hand - these are the building blocks of a caring and supportive community.

Throughout our lives, we meet moments where we can extend a helping hand to those around us. Sometimes, it's as effortless as offering a genuine compliment to a coworker who's been feeling stressed. Other times, it might be listening without judgment to a friend going through a difficult time.

In the unspoken method, we see that the true power of HELP lies not only in the act itself but in its intention. It's about approaching every interaction with empathy and a willingness to be present for one another.

As we journey further into the realm of HELP, we'll explore the different sides of this unspoken kindness. We'll delve into the art of encouraging others, supporting them in their endeavours, and upholding their dignity. And through it all, we'll discover that in helping others, we also help ourselves grow and connect with the very essence of being human.

So, let us embark on this chapter together, hand in hand, as we explore the profound impact of HELP in the unspoken method and embrace the transformative power of unspoken kindness in our lives.

In the heart of the chapter on HELP, we find a pragmatic and practical approach that embodies the principles of the unspoken method. Helping others becomes a natural extension of our daily lives, where kindness and support flow effortlessly.

To encourage is to be a positive force in someone's life, providing motivation and reassurance. By offering encouragement, we uplift their spirits and instil confidence in their abilities.

Support becomes a pillar of strength, creating a safety net for those who need it. Whether lending a hand with a task or being there to listen, support is the backbone of a caring and compassionate community.

Upholding the dignity of others means treating everyone with respect and empathy. It's about seeing the value in each person and acknowledging their worth, regardless of their background or circumstances.

In the unspoken method, we understand that helping others isn't a burden or an obligation; it's an opportunity for growth and connection. Extending a helping hand creates a positive ripple effect that spreads through our relationships and communities.

So, let us encourage and support one another in our endeavours, celebrating each other's successes and providing comfort during challenging times. By upholding the dignity of every individual, we foster a culture of inclusivity and understanding.

The essence of HELP is in the small acts of kindness we perform daily. From a simple compliment to a lending ear, these gestures can brighten someone's day and make a lasting impact.

As we embrace the unspoken method of HELP, we recognise that we are all interconnected, and our actions have the potential to make a difference. So, let's infuse our lives with encouragement, support, and upholding and watch as the world transforms into a place of compassion and unity.

PART FOUR

MOBILISING A MENTALLY FIT WORKFORCE: EMBRACING HELP, IMPLEMENTING THE UNSPOKEN METHOD

> "Our task must be to free ourselves... by widening our circle of compassion to embrace all living creatures and the whole of nature and it's beauty."
> — Albert Einstein

Aligning Purpose and Action in the Workplace

In the earlier chapters, we explored the power of embracing help and the significance of leading with purpose to promote mental health in the workplace. Now, it's time to delve into the practical implementation of the Unspoken Method—the HOW that can mobilise a mentally healthy workforce.

Aligning Purpose and Action is the pivotal bridge between intention and impact. To create a workplace culture that fosters mental well-being, we must ensure that our actions align with the values and purpose we aim to embody. Here's how we can make it happen:

Uncover the Unspoken: Active Listening and Effective Communication

A fundamental aspect of the Unspoken Method is the art of active listening and effective communication. Many times, people may feel hesitant to express their struggles openly. As leaders and colleagues, we create a safe space for genuine and transparent conversations.

Active listening goes beyond hearing words; it involves giving our full attention, understanding the emotions behind the comments, and showing empathy. When someone reaches out for help or shares their challenges, being fully present without judgment is essential. By listening actively, we communicate that their well-being matters to us and confirm their experiences.

Cultivate Psychological Safety

To embrace help in the workplace, we must cultivate psychological safety. In this culture, employees feel comfortable speaking up, taking risks, and being vulnerable. This sense of security stems from leaders fostering an environment that values openness and compassion.

Leaders must model vulnerability and be willing to share their struggles to show that seeking help is not a sign of weakness. When employees see this behaviour in their leaders, they are more likely to feel safe seeking support.

Promote Resource Accessibility

Ensure that workplace mental health resources are easily accessible. Implement employee assistance programs, mental health workshops, and counselling services, and make information on these resources readily available.

By promoting resource accessibility, we communicate that seeking help is accepted and supported. Additionally, consider offering flexible work arrangements to accommodate employees' well-being needs.

Break Down Stigmas

Stigmas surrounding mental health can hinder individuals from seeking help. We must engage in continuous awareness and education efforts to break down these barriers.

Host workshops and training sessions to provide a deeper understanding of mental health challenges and how to support colleagues who might be experiencing them. Encourage open discussions about mental health, aiming to destigmatise seeking help and promote a culture of empathy and compassion.

Encourage Peer Support

Creating a peer support network is a powerful way to embrace help in the workplace. Encourage employees to look out for one another and offer support when needed.

Implement mentorship programs and support groups where colleagues can connect, share experiences, and offer guidance. Peer support can foster a sense of community, reducing feelings of isolation and strengthening the bonds between team members.

Celebrate Vulnerability and Growth

Finally, celebrate vulnerability and growth within the organisation. Recognise and appreciate individuals who have sought help, shared their struggles, and demonstrated resilience.

When we celebrate vulnerability and growth, we reinforce that seeking help is a courageous act that leads to personal and professional development. This affirmation empowers others to embrace support without fear of judgment.

Implementing the HOW: A Call to Action

As we step into the realm of implementing the HOW, let us be intentional in our actions. Aligning purpose and activity means living the values of the Unspoken Method in our daily interactions. By fostering a culture of active listening, psychological safety, and resource accessibility, we create a thriving workplace that prioritises mental well-being.

Every small step brings the Unspoken Method to life, mobilising a mentally healthy workforce that supports and uplifts one another. Let this be our call to action—a shared commitment to embrace help and create a brighter, more compassionate future for everyone in the workplace. Together, we can make it happen.

HOPE - ILLUMINATING THE PATH AHEAD IN THE UNSPOKEN METHOD

"It's really a wonder that I haven't dropped all my ideals, because they seem so absurd and impossible to carry out. Yet I keep them, because in spite of everything, I still believe that people are really good at heart."
— Anne Frank, The Diary of a Young Girl

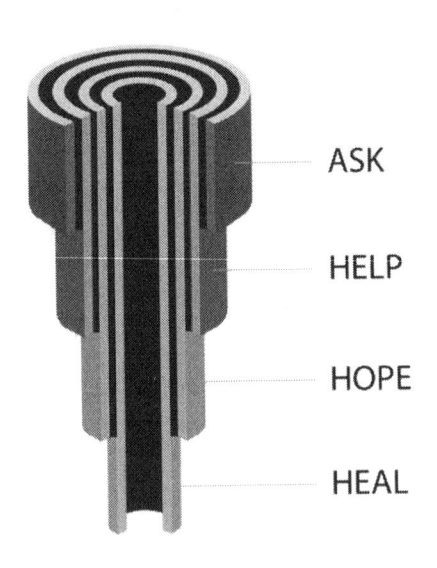

- ASK
- HELP
- HOPE
- HEAL

Having taken the first courageous step of asking for help, we now venture into the realm of hope. This force shall illuminate the path ahead in the unspoken method. Just as we navigated the intricate labyrinth of seeking help, we shall now delve into the transformative power of hope in the world of work. As we appear from the shadows of fear and hesitation, we find ourselves on the threshold of a profound revelation: hope, like a guiding star, can lead us through the darkest times. It is the unwavering belief that there is a glimmer of light even in the bleakest of circumstances—a belief that fuels resilience, perseverance, and the unyielding determination to overcome. So, let us embark on this journey of hope, knowing that together, we can thrive through the unspoken method.

The Unyielding Power of Hope: Thriving Through the Unspoken Method

Stress and hope engage in an eternal battle for supremacy in the vast work landscape. As we navigate the trials and tribulations of our professional lives, we often find ourselves wading through turbulent waters, facing challenges that threaten to drown us in despair. In these moments, hope emerges as a beacon of light, guiding us through the darkness.

In the annals of psychological exploration, Curt Richter's experiment on drowning rats resounds as a stark testament to the power of hope and resilience. Though unsettling, its findings reveal a profound truth: Hope can be the lifeblood that sustains us in the face of seemingly insurmountable obstacles.

In these experiments, rats were placed in buckets filled with water to see how long they could survive. The findings were both poignant and illuminating. Domesticated rats reacted differently to the water. Some swam around exploring, while others opted to stay near the surface, paddling tirelessly. The former succumbed to exhaustion in mere minutes, but the latter, driven by an indomitable hope, survived for days.

Next, wild rats, known for their aggression and superior swimming abilities, were introduced to the buckets. Despite their ferocity, each one met a swift demise, unable to endure the ordeal for more than a few minutes. Curt Richter astutely recognised that hope played a pivotal role in this harrowing trial.

The rats that clung to the surface with tenacious hope had, in their ways, experienced salvation before. This prior taste of rescue fuelled their determination to keep fighting, believing that not all was lost. However, unfamiliar with such hope, the wild rats quickly succumbed to despair.

The turning point came when Curt offered the rats hope and support. He saved them just before they drowned, helped them recover, and then placed them back into the buckets. The result was astounding—the rats swam far longer than before, for they had tasted hope, a lifeline to a brighter future.

What can we humans glean from this peculiar yet impactful experiment? While our experiences differ vastly from those of rats, we share a common thread—the tenacity of hope. We exhibit higher levels of perseverance and resilience when we hold onto hope. Just as the rescued rats found strength in believing their situation was not entirely hopeless, we can also muster the willpower to brave the storms that beset us.

In the world of work, hope assumes an even more profound significance. A glimmer of hope takes root when leaders provide their teams with a vision of a better future. With this hope as an anchor, individuals can weather the most challenging circumstances, knowing they are not alone in their struggle. Hope breeds unity, support, and a collective spirit—a workforce primed to triumph over adversity.

So, as we navigate the unspoken method, we must remember the resilient drowning rats. They illuminate the truth that hope is not a mere sentiment but a force that empowers us to endure, thrive, and forge a path toward a better tomorrow. As we dare to rescue each other from despair, we kindle the flames of hope, and together, we shall prevail through the unspoken method.

Like the rats in Curt's experiment, we, too, can find ourselves immersed in circumstances that evoke a sense of hopelessness. The unforgiving pressures of the workplace, the weight of responsibilities, and the uncertainty of the future may tempt us to surrender to the currents of despair.

Yet, hope is not an abstract concept reserved for philosophical ponderings. It is an actionable force we can nurture and extend to those around us. It is the belief that a flicker of light remains even amidst the darkest times.

In the world of work, hope can take many forms. It appears when we experience the warmth of support from colleagues and leaders who extend a helping hand, pulling us from the brink of despair. Like the rats given hope through rescue and support, our perseverance thrives when we know we are not alone in our struggles.

Leaders bear the unique responsibility of fostering hope in their teams. Creating a culture of care and compassion provides a fertile ground for hope to take root. When leaders offer support, demonstrate belief in their team members, and instil a sense of purpose, hope springs forth, and with it, the resilience to withstand adversity.

As we contemplate the implications of the drowning rat's experiment in the context of the world of work, we recognise the profound impact hope can have on our collective well-being. It is a force that empowers us to weather the storms, face challenges head-on, and envision a brighter future.

Let us recognise the importance of hope in our professional lives. Let us remember that hope is not a luxury but a necessity. By embracing hope and extending it to one another, we embody the essence of the unspoken method. We become a community bound by empathy, compassion, and a shared belief in the power of hope.

Through the unspoken method, we unravel the enigma of stress and disempower its hold on us. We build a fortress of hope from which we draw strength, resilience, and the courage to persevere. As we move forward, let us harness the unyielding power of hope and walk together, united in our pursuit of a future where stress retreats and hope reigns supreme.

In the depths of darkness and pain, as I write these words, my heart is still aching from the recent passing of my father. I find myself drawn to something far more hopeful. I celebrate his life, which intertwined with mine in the most unexpected ways.

At the tender age of eleven, I had grown up in a single-parent house. My biological dad didn't want me, and I have never seen or heard from him.

This situation was complicated, and I grew up feeling profound rejection, which caused a lot of adult co-dependency traits that needed work to overcome, with very little money and resources, a void that left me carrying wounds of rejection and anger. It was tough.

But my father, though imperfect, made a choice that altered my course. He took me under his care, choosing to become my dad and weaving himself into the tapestry of my life, guiding me with his strict yet honest presence.

He had a mysterious and awe-inspiring past, having served in special forces and clandestine operations. His journey in the oil and gas industry spanned twenty years, and he led with expertise and a remarkable sense of pride. His experiences inspired not just me but my brothers and nephew, all of us following his footsteps into the industry he loved.

As my brother and I stood before the draw works from the Murchison, a piece of history where our father had worked, I felt a gentle moment of hope. It was as if my father's legacy, his reaching out to me as a child, had paved the way for my journey through the armed forces, my service to my country, and my pursuit of a better self in the energy industry.

Although my path has taken a different turn, I am now more than ever infused with inspired hope. My passion lies in communication and connecting with people, and in writing this book, I extend my hand in hope, reaching out to you and others and fostering a better place for all who seek help.

I dedicate this chapter to my father, a great man who left an indelible mark on my life. In his honour, I carry a torch of hope, a belief in the power of asking, helping, and finding that calling that ignites hope in our hearts.

May you feel the presence of good men and women striving to improve the world. Together, through the unspoken method, we shall weave a tapestry of hope and support, where we embrace each other's struggles and triumphs, knowing that hope lives within the power of asking and that we have the strength to rise and shine brighter than ever before. All we need to do is ask.

EMBRACING HELP: TH
OF A STRONGER LEADER

"In the depth of winter, I finally learned that within me there lay an invincible summer."
— Albert Camus

Picture this: You find yourself at work, faced with a daunting task that seems way beyond your ability. Your heart races, and that stubborn voice warns you not to ask for help. After all, won't it make you look weak?

Vicky, a successful executive, shared her fears with us. Despite her impressive career growth, she still needed to prepare for her responsibilities. Vicky was scared to admit she needed help, afraid of appearing inadequate. But you know what happened when she did reach out? It wasn't weakness that defined her; it was courage.

You see, asking for help is often seen as a sign of vulnerability. We fear it will expose our limitations and tarnish our image as capable leaders. But embracing support can transform us into more robust, more effective leaders. Let's uncover the power of this act through four compelling reasons:

...th through Discomfort

Asking for help means stepping outside our comfort zones. And yes, it can be uncomfortable, even scary. But it's precisely in that discomfort that growth happens. The Unspoken Method reminds us that facing challenges that stretch us is okay. Embracing pain is like flexing a muscle—strengthening us for future endeavours.

Preserving Our Greatest Asset

We all have our limits. Taking on too much can lead to burnout and diminished performance. By seeking assistance, we protect our most valuable asset: ourselves. It's not about weakness—it's about recognising our boundaries and ensuring we stay effective in the long run.

Unleashing Diverse Perspectives

Some say asking for help makes us look weak, but let me tell you a secret: award-winning leaders often seek advice from outside their immediate circles. It's true! When we embrace help, we unlock a treasure trove of diverse insights and ideas. This fresh perspective can lead to solutions we wouldn't have thought of alone.

Empowering Our Team

Imagine this: You're a leader asking your team for their input. What does it communicate? Trust, appreciation, and empowerment. Embracing helps show your colleagues that their ideas matter and that they are valued team members. It fosters a culture of collaboration and camaraderie.

So, here's the bottom line: Asking for help is not a sign of weakness. It's a bold step toward growth, more decisive leadership, and team cohesion. When we dare to seek help, we create a supportive work environment that nurtures mental health and fosters success.

Remember Vicky? Once she embraced help, she felt a weight lift off her shoulders. She saw the transformational impact it brought to her leadership journey. You can experience that too. Embrace help, and watch yourself and your team thrive, positively impacting your workplace. So, don't hesitate to see the difference it makes. You've got this!

PART FIVE

NAVIGATING WORKPLACE MENTAL HEALTH CHALLENGES

"Life throws challenges and every challenge comes with rainbows and lights to conquer it."
— Amit Ray, *World Peace: The Voice of a Mountain Bird*

Managing Organisational Disconnects

In an ideal world, the workplace would be a nurturing space where mental health is openly acknowledged and supported. Unfortunately, we often find ourselves in environments where this is different. Navigating the complexities of the unspoken method can be challenging, but it's not impossible. Here are some strategies to help you overcome workplace mental health obstacles:

Breaking The Silence

If your workplace culture tends to stigmatise mental health discussions, it's time to break the silence. Find allies who share your concerns and start conversations about mental well-being. You can slowly shift the culture towards greater acceptance and support by initiating open dialogues.

Creating Safe Spaces

In an environment where mental health is not openly addressed, creating safe spaces becomes crucial. Encourage informal gatherings or support groups where colleagues can share their challenges without fear of judgment. When we come together with empathy and understanding, we foster a sense of belonging that promotes mental well-being. This is achieved by speaking. You're not expected to shout from the office window or rooftops. What I mean by speaking is having a meaningful conversation with a trusted work colleague about something which matters to you both, and from their point of view, you can be a kind and gentle listener, which empowers them to speak from a place of truth. It may seem slightly scary, but you will quickly find people ready for this level of openness in your workforce.

Influencing From Within

If you are influential in your organisation, leverage it to advocate for mental health initiatives. Champion policies that prioritise employee well-being and foster a healthy work-life balance. Leading with purpose and empathy can inspire positive change and demonstrate the power of a mentally healthy workplace.

Self-Care And Boundaries

In challenging workplace environments, it's essential to prioritise self-care and set healthy boundaries. Recognise when work-related stress is taking a toll on your mental health and be unapologetic in seeking the support you need. Embrace the unspoken method of embracing help and reach out to trusted friends or professionals if necessary. Healing is not some woo-woo subject these days. It's as or, if not more important than, the company values and vision. You can heal or rectify bottom-line revenue and profits with healthy, open-minded communication. Candour is worth its weight in gold and should be based on genuine empathy, not pushy profit tactics. The days of an industrial-level mindset are over; we must focus on a healthy workforce that cares about each other. Healing is powerful and can massively improve your sales and revenue. Which is always great news.

The Power of Leading by Example

Remember, change starts with you. By embracing the unspoken method, we can lead by example and encourage others to do the same. Share your experiences, talk about your journey towards mental well-being, and let others know it's okay to seek help. Your vulnerability can inspire a ripple effect that transforms the workplace culture. This is the power of healing in a working environment, and it can make you and your brand grow new life into its blood.

Patience And Persistence

Overcoming workplace mental health challenges is not an overnight endeavour. It requires patience and persistence. Be prepared for resistance or setbacks but stay committed to your mission. Small steps can lead to significant shifts; every effort towards a mentally healthy workplace is worth it.

In conclusion, navigating workplace mental health challenges within the unspoken method can be demanding. Still, it's a journey worth embarking on. We can positively change our workplaces by breaking the silence, creating safe spaces, influencing change, prioritising self-care, leading by example, and supporting persistence. Remember, mental health matters and your efforts to foster a supportive environment will benefit you, your colleagues, and the entire organisation. Together, let's embrace the unspoken method and create workplaces that prioritise the well-being and healing of everyone involved.

HEAL – THE FINAL STEP IN THE UNSPOKEN METHOD

"Scars have the strange power to remind us that our past is real."
— Cormac McCarthy, All the Pretty Horses

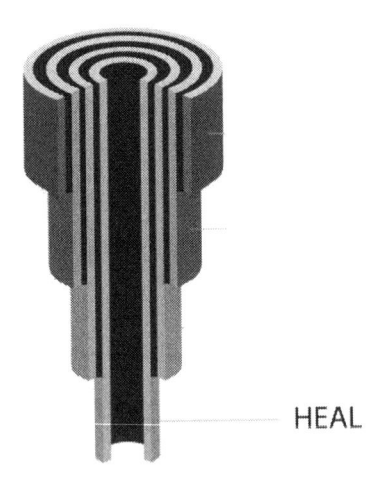

HEAL

Speaking is Healing: Healing the Unspoken Wounds Through The Transformative Power of Speaking.

In the depths of our struggles, we have explored the power of asking for help and the glimmer of hope that can ignite resilience within us. As we journey through the unspoken method, we arrive at the heart of our healing.

What is the true meaning of healing? To make free from injury or disease; to make sound or whole; to restore health. Healing is not merely the mending of physical wounds but a profound journey of restoration and renewal, encompassing the body, mind, and soul.

In our world of work, we often encounter injuries that are not visible to the naked eye. The weight of stress, anxiety, and burnout takes a toll on you, manifesting in ways that can go unnoticed, unacknowledged, and unaddressed. Yet, as you embrace the unspoken method, you acknowledge that speaking is healing.

We open ourselves to the power of vulnerability through gentle empathy and compassion. In sharing our struggles, we begin to mend the invisible wounds that may have long been tucked away in the recesses of our hearts. Speaking invites understanding, support, and a sense of belonging, a reminder that we are not alone in our journey.

Let us embark on this chapter of healing with a profound understanding that healing is not a linear path. It is a winding road filled with ups and downs, but with each step forward, we grow stronger. Together, we shall navigate through the pain, the darkness, and the uncertainties, illuminating the way with the light of compassion and the warmth of connection.

In gentle empathy, we find the courage to confront our wounds, tend to the scars, and embrace the beauty of our imperfections. As we heal, we uncover a strength that may have gone unnoticed, a resilience that sustains us through trials and tribulations.

Let this chapter of healing be a sanctuary of solace and understanding. May it remind us that speaking is healing, and in the unspoken method, we find a tapestry of support woven by the threads of vulnerability and empathy.

Together, let us embark on this transformative journey of healing, knowing that in seeking help, embracing hope, and speaking our truths, we create a sacred space for growth, resilience, and a future that radiates with the light of healing.

In the Embrace of Vulnerability: Caitlin's Journey of Healing and Hope After Her Father's Suicide

Sitting across from Caitlin in the podcast studio of WOUNDED, I braced myself to broach a sensitive and dark topic—her father's suicide and the aftermath that followed. It was evident that the wounds were still raw, as one would expect after such a tragic loss. Yet, despite the gravity of the conversation, Caitlin exuded a presence filled with energy and compassion, touching closer to hope than darkness.

Her words flowed with positivity and authenticity, allowing her to speak candidly about the most challenging moment of her life. However, what struck me most was her fervent passion for sharing her story. Caitlin's courage to be vulnerable was remarkable in a world discouraging openness about wounds and mental health struggles.

As I listened intently to her journey and its impact on her family, I felt transported into her world, granted a brief glimpse into her heart. Embracing vulnerability in the presence of another person is not only a sign of strength but a profoundly human experience.

Recently, I came across a podcast where a man spoke about the brevity of life and death. Death, he described, is brutal and cold, mirrored in our notions of strength—steadfast and unyielding. Conversely, life flows gently like water, moving around and through us without trying to force or pull us. It simply exists, always present, waiting for us to immerse ourselves in its flow.

Like a leaf or flower, life is soft and beautiful when alive, but as it nears the end, it becomes hard and brittle, eventually breaking apart. Even a cat, when falling from a tree, instinctively becomes floppy and soft, cushioning the impact of the hard ground.

And so, life demands that we embrace its gentleness and softness, just as Caitlin did when she spoke of her father. She showed calmness, consideration, and, above all, an abundance of love and empathy for him.

In contrast, I've often witnessed children becoming bitter towards parents who died from suicide. But I believe we are moving towards a world where discussing hard things openly is becoming possible. Caitlin, acting as a beacon of hope for me, can extend the same hope to others. Her story can inspire courage in troubled times to ask for help and find hope within themselves.

With courage, we can start to heal and, most importantly, learn to speak about our pain. Embracing vulnerability and seeking support can lead to profound healing, not just of the past, but also a brighter, more connected future. Caitlin's journey exemplifies the transformative power of healing through sharing, and it reminds us that life, with its joys and struggles, beckons us to be present, gentle, and alive.

Unmasking the Enemy: Confronting the Tyranny of Stress

An insidious enemy lurks in our fast-paced, high-pressure world, preying upon our well-being, relationships, and productivity. Its name is stress. It's a foe that knows no boundaries, sparing no one in its relentless pursuit of conquest. Its ubiquitous presence and effects are far-reaching, leaving no aspect of our lives untouched.

Stress is not an ephemeral visitor who knocks on our door and departs with a fleeting visit. No, it lingers, persistently lurking in the shadows, ready to ambush us at any moment. When stress overstays its welcome, it creates a cascade of physical, emotional, and behavioural disturbances, turning our lives into battlefields.

In this chapter, we bravely confront the enemy within. We face the stark reality of stress's reign and acknowledge its toll on our bodies, minds, and relationships. From the somatic manifestations of headaches and muscle tension to the silent assailant raising our blood pressure and weakening our immunity – stress wages war on our physical health.

Yet, its grasp doesn't stop there. With cunning precision, stress infiltrates the sanctum of our minds, corroding our mental health. It lays the groundwork for anxiety, depression, and a myriad of mood disorders while stoking the embers of existing mental health conditions, threatening to engulf us in darkness.

Sleep, a sanctuary for the weary soul, becomes yet another battleground. Stress disrupts its tranquillity, robbing us of restful slumber. The consequences are dire – fatigue, irritability, and further deterioration of our physical and mental well-being.

Unabated stress launches an assault on our cognitive abilities. Our once-sharp minds become clouded, decision-making falters, and concentration becomes elusive. Simple tasks turn into Herculean feats, leaving us feeling overwhelmed and incapable.

In relationships, stress plays the role of a puppeteer, pulling the strings of conflict and communication breakdowns. As the tension mounts, we may find ourselves isolated, battling the hardships alone while our connections fray.

The impact of stress is not confined to the individual; it spills over into the professional realm. Our work becomes a battleground, with stress as the saboteur. Productivity wanes, absenteeism soars, and the spectre of burnout looms ever closer.

To cope with this relentless adversary, some seek refuge in unhealthy vices – alcohol, drugs, food, anger, resentment, jealousy, or other harmful means – only to find themselves further ensnared in the clutches of addictive or dangerous activities.

But there is hope amidst this struggle. The path to liberation begins with acknowledgement and open dialogue. We must break the silence and speak of stress not as a sign of weakness but as an epidemic that affects us all. By sharing our stories, we dispel the stigma surrounding stress and unite in our fight against this common enemy.

In the unspoken method, we stand together, hand in hand, a united front against stress. We equip ourselves with healthy coping strategies forged from resilience and strength. In reaching out for help, we demonstrate courage and vulnerability, dispelling the notion that self-reliance is the only path.

As we face the reality of stress, let us remember that we are not alone. Together, we stand tall, an army of compassion and empathy, supporting one another through the storm. By addressing stress head-on and fostering an environment of understanding and care, we pave the way to a brighter, more resilient future that thrives on unity and shared humanity.

I have delved deep into the movement of healing, speaking openly about my wounds and extending a helping hand to countless individuals facing various life challenges. From prisons to veterans, energy executives to oil and gas workers, men and women to struggling teenagers, I have witnessed the transformative power of healing and the impact of sharing our stories.

Initially feeling alone in the darkness, I embarked on my healing journey without formal training. However, I consciously embraced the shadows and used the torch to navigate my wounds. I documented and shared my fight, failures, and successes with others along the way. This experience led me to recognise that we all possess an inherent power and wisdom within our wounds.

This realisation shaped the essence of my podcast, WOUNDED, where I've engaged with thousands of people over the years. Through these conversations, I've firmly believed that healing begins with speaking. We create a profound connection with others when we courageously share our stories and open up about our struggles. By allowing others to witness our journey, we offer strength and encouragement to the present moment.

Courage does not precede the act; instead, it emerges at the end of the fight. By facing our fears, we gain the energy to overcome the challenges. In this process, we inspire others to do the same and create a supportive community where we can learn from each other's experiences.

The simple act of speaking and sharing our truths can ignite a healing chain reaction. It empowers others to find solace in their vulnerabilities and fosters a sense of camaraderie in our shared struggles. In this collective healing journey, we uncover the potential for growth, resilience, and hope.

Ultimately, the unspoken method of embracing help, vulnerability, and openness paves the way for profound healing in ourselves and others. Together, we can journey towards a future where healing is a personal endeavour and a collective experience that connects us on a profoundly human level.

Unmasking Suppressed Emotions: The Importance of Emotional Openness

In a world that often values stoicism and emotional restraint, it's no surprise that many individuals find themselves suppressing their feelings and emotions. However, as our understanding of mental health evolves, it's becoming increasingly apparent that emotional openness is an essential component of overall well-being. By not allowing ourselves the freedom to express our emotions, we may inadvertently increase our stress levels, anxiety, and susceptibility to other mental health challenges.

I remember feeling like this when I left the army. The pressure to make meaning was more formidable than I wished for, and I felt detached from what mattered. Struggling to secure a sure footing every day was a fight to handle even the simplest of emotions, which led me to a dark and disastrous downfall. Sharing my feelings was a sign of weakness and unmanliness. I kept my front and mask up high and pushed myself into the void of self-pity. I pretended to handle the days, nights, or weeks of work without that feeling I once held of service to a calling more significant than myself. Later on, after I began my journey of healing, I realised it was me who was the force of negativity and had bound me to this place.

There is honour in all work, from stacking shelves and sorting mail to fixing harbours and sailing the seas for fish. All work is honourable, but holding onto the idea that we must live stoically in every way where we never connect with each other is the fastest road to ruin. We need a realistic pathway to allow expression to be heard and noticed.

Suppressed emotions can manifest in various ways, both mentally and physically. When we don't allow ourselves to express our feelings, we may experience increased stress and anxiety. Over time, this constant state of tension can lead to burnout, depression, and other mental health issues. Furthermore, the strain of suppressed emotions can also manifest in physical symptoms such as headaches, muscle tension, or gastrointestinal problems. These physical symptoms indicate that our emotional well-being is intrinsically linked to our overall health.

To counteract the negative consequences of suppressed emotions, it's essential to cultivate a culture of emotional openness in our personal and professional lives. By encouraging open communication and fostering an environment where individuals feel safe sharing their thoughts and feelings, we can help alleviate the burden of suppressed emotions.

One way to encourage emotional openness is by practising active listening. When we genuinely listen to others and try to understand their feelings, we create an atmosphere of trust and empathy. This trust encourages individuals to share their emotions more openly and honestly, which can lead to stronger connections and improved well-being.

As Simon Sinek says, "Leadership is not about being in charge. It's about taking care of those in your charge." In a world that encourages toughness and independence, it can be challenging to embrace vulnerability. However, when we share our emotions and experiences, we demonstrate to others that being open and honest about our feelings is okay. This can help break down barriers and encourage others to express their emotions.

The following stories will inspire you to feel and express yourself with sensitivity, enriching your place of work by listening to others and sharing personal moments. We don't have to gush our hearts out to grow as a team. We just need to know that we have each other's backs and will not judge one another when our opening moment arrives.

In conclusion, emotional openness is crucial to mental health and overall well-being. We can help by fostering a culture of openness and encouraging individuals to express their emotions.

The alchemy of healing through speaking is a wondrous transformation when we summon the courage to share our truth with others. Speaking, in all its forms—conversations, storytelling, or sharing our experiences through platforms like podcasts—becomes a superpower that has the potential to uplift, connect, and heal us all.

When we speak, we embark on a journey of vulnerability, a path illuminated by the wisdom of Brene Brown. In those opening moments, we shed the weight of secrecy and shame, releasing the emotions and experiences festering within. This act of vulnerability is not a sign of weakness; instead, it takes immense strength to lay bare our fears, struggles, and scars before others. I am terrified to write this book, afraid of rejection and being mocked by my peers if there are poorly written parts or grammar errors, but to fail is to be human. To make mistakes is to be alive. And so, I embrace this side of myself. I am not so afraid that I stay rigid, unable to act or try to make a difference through my experience. And I invite you to do the same. It's liberating to live your life with mistakes. They make you who you are. And even open you up to the wisdom in your wounds.

We transmute pain into connection through speaking, echoing Simon Sinek's teachings. As we share our stories, we find that our experiences are not unique; they resonate with the human experience. Our vulnerabilities become bridges that connect us to others, fostering empathy and understanding. The power of these connections cannot be underestimated—they can heal and uplift individuals and entire communities.

When we speak, we rewrite the narrative of strength. Rather than hiding behind the mask of perfection, we embrace the beauty of imperfection. We break free from the constraints of societal expectations and allow ourselves to be authentic and genuine. This liberation frees us from the burden of trying to be someone we are not, giving us the space to embrace our true selves.

Speaking is a declaration of self-worth and self-love. By giving voice to our experiences, we acknowledge that our stories matter. We validate our emotions and honour our journey. In doing so, we recognise that we deserve love, compassion, and support.

Moreover, speaking ignites a ripple effect of healing. When we courageously speak, we inspire others to do the same. Our vulnerability creates a safe space for others to share their struggles, creating a chain reaction of openness and support. In this interconnected web of healing, we become healers for ourselves and each other.

Embracing the superpower of speaking, we discover the beauty of resilience. Through storytelling, we find strength in our past, courage in the present, and hope for the future. Our words become agents of transformation, offering solace and guidance to those navigating similar challenges.

As we navigate the complexities of the modern world, speaking becomes a compass that guides us through the storm. It empowers us to navigate the uncharted waters of our emotions and experiences, helping us find direction, purpose, and meaning. Our voices become the light that pierces through the darkness, illuminating the path to healing and growth.

In essence, speaking is an act of self-empowerment, a celebration of our inherent worthiness as human beings. It is a force that unites us, transcending borders and barriers reminding us of the universality of our shared humanity. In the alchemy of healing through speaking, we discover our true strength, which lies in our capacity to connect, heal, and thrive as one.

In the sacred dance of healing, we find the unspoken method has led us to a profound revelation—the power of speaking and the magic of vulnerability. With each shared story and every heartfelt conversation, we weave a tapestry of connection that binds us together.

In a world that once shunned open conversations about mental health and struggles, we now stand at a turning point—a moment where we collectively embrace the transformative force of speaking. Through podcasts, like water softly flowing, we break down the barriers of silence that once separated us. Listeners feel seen and understood, uniting in empathy transcending the boundaries of geography, culture, and time.

As we step into the dance of vulnerability, we invite the healing light to permeate every corner of our lives. We share our stories, shed our masks, and embrace the tenderness of being human. Through this collective awakening, we create a world where speaking is healing, compassion reigns, and the power of our voices unites us in strength and resilience.

In the closing of this chapter, I extend an embrace—a gentle reminder that healing awaits each of us when we find the courage to speak. Your voice matters, and your story carries the potential to ignite healing in yourself and others. As we journey forward, let us be torchbearers of hope and beacons of light for one another.

May we, like Caitlin, be the beacons of hope for one another—guiding each other towards the courage to speak, heal, and transform our world into a sanctuary of empathy and understanding.

Together, we rise. Together, we heal. Together, we speak. Let us embrace this unspoken method and embark on a healing, compassion, and transformation journey. The world awaits the magic of your voice.

PART SIX

DISCOVERING PURPOSE FOR WORKPLACE MENTAL HEALTH

> "What should young people do with their lives today? Many things, obviously. But the most daring thing is to create stable communities in which the terrible disease of loneliness can be cured."
> — Kurt Vonnegut

The Roots of Purpose-Driven Mental Health

In the journey of the unspoken method, we have delved into the depths of healing, explored the power of vulnerability, and navigated the complexities of workplace challenges. Now, we arrive at a pivotal point where purpose intersects with mental health in the workplace.

Purpose is the compass that guides us through the storms of stress and uncertainty. The fuel ignites our passion and drives us to persevere when the path ahead seems obscured. As we embrace the unspoken method and the art of speaking, we discover the roots of purpose-driven mental health and intertwine them in a tapestry of hope and resilience.

The first thread in this tapestry is the realisation that purpose is not an elusive concept reserved for a chosen few. Each of us carries within the seeds of purpose, waiting to bloom and flourish in the right environment.

In my heart, I've wholeheartedly embraced this purpose – the belief that our wounds hold seeds of wisdom waiting to bloom with the proper nourishment and care. Rather than hindering us, these wounds provide the sustenance we need to evolve into better versions of ourselves. Why? Because the ever-increasing levels of stress and burnout demand that we come together to face each day's challenges and anxieties. If we allow ourselves to be suppressed by these pressures, we risk living in a state of subjugation. But I refuse to accept such an existence. My passion is to inspire others with this very ideal.

I know it's not easy; nothing worthwhile in life ever is. However, I want you to see that there is a path through all this stress. It lies in opening up and speaking about your own experiences, releasing some pressure from your journey and the lives of those who work alongside you. By sharing your struggles and allowing vulnerability, you create a space where others can do the same, forming a supportive and empathetic network.

Together, through the unspoken method of speaking and listening, we can uplift one another and nurture our mental health. Let us embrace our wounds, shared humanity, and collective growth potential. Through this joint effort, we can break free from the shackles of stress, find healing in vulnerability, and create a workplace that values mental well-being above all else.

In the workplace, purpose-driven mental health means creating a culture that nurtures these seeds, allowing individuals to connect their values and aspirations with the organisation's broader mission.

When purpose takes root, competition transforms into collaboration. The fear of judgment dissipates, replaced by the camaraderie of shared goals. Instead of competing against each other, we collaborate to achieve collective success, supporting one another in our quests for growth and innovation.

Purpose-driven mental health does not ignore the challenges or pretend they do not exist. Instead, it harnesses the power of communication, allowing individuals to speak up about their struggles without fear of judgment. When we openly share our vulnerabilities and seek help through the unspoken method, we create a workplace where healing is not a weakness but a strength.

Leaders play a pivotal role in this new frontier of purpose-driven mental health. They understand that their influence extends beyond the bottom line, reaching deep into the hearts and minds of their team members. With empathy and compassion, they inspire their workforce to embrace the unspoken method, to listen and support one another, and to foster an environment where everyone's voice is valued.

As individuals, we discover that our purpose is not confined to the boundaries of our job titles. Purpose-driven mental health ignites a passion for lifelong learning and personal growth. We seek opportunities to expand our knowledge, to embrace challenges that take us out of our comfort zones, and to develop a deeper understanding of ourselves and others.

As we weave purpose and mental health together, we recognise that the unspoken method is not just about speaking but also about listening. We listen to ourselves, acknowledging our inner struggles and needs. We listen to our colleagues, offering empathy and understanding. We listen to the organisation's heartbeat, aligning our efforts with its broader purpose.

With the unspoken method as our guide, we embark on a collective journey of healing and growth, bonded by our shared commitment to purpose-driven mental health. The tapestry we weave becomes a testament to the power of speaking and listening, the strength of vulnerability, and the beauty of resilience.

In the workplace of tomorrow, purpose and mental health walk hand in hand, illuminating the path to a brighter and more compassionate future. Let us carry this torch of hope, lighting the way for others to find their missing piece in this stressful world. Let us stand united, ready to heal through speaking, and thrive in purposeful, compassionate collaboration.

THE POWER OF OPENNESS: EMBRACING THE WISDOM IN THE WOUND

"The worst wounds, the deadliest of them, aren't the ones people see on the outside. They're the ones that make us bleed internally."
— Sherrilyn Kenyon, Infamous

In our society, we often learn to hide our wounds to project an image of strength and invincibility. But what if we changed our perspective and embraced the power of openness, vulnerability, and transformation? What if we saw our wounds not as signs of weakness but as catalysts for growth and change?

Embracing my wounds was a profound journey. It shattered the false notion that I needed to be tough and macho. Instead, it allowed me to connect with my vulnerability, creating a more profound sense of compassion and empathy. It opened me up to my true self, enabling me to fully feel, laugh, and love. A path of growth and humility connected me to the essence of culture itself. It was the discovery of the wisdom in the wound.

Simon Sinek and Cornel West both emphasise the significance of openness and vulnerability in creating meaningful change within and in the world around us. Sinek talks about "starting with why," connecting with our deeper purpose to inspire action. West urges us to confront uncomfortable truths and embrace discomfort to foster a more just and compassionate world.

At the core of their ideas lies the concept of openness. By opening ourselves up to our wounds, vulnerabilities, and most profound truths, we create space for growth, healing, and transformation. Empathy and understanding flourish when we share our stories and connect with others with similar experiences. Our wounds become a shared human experience rather than sources of shame.

I won't ask you to be brave or to shout about your mental health and well-being. We are bombarded with noise in that arena. Instead, I invite you to embrace a culture of openness and gentleness. Speak from the heart, but do so at your own pace, understanding that not everyone feels compelled to share openly. We have diverse personalities, and the spectrum of philosophical decency in our communities and culture should be acknowledged and celebrated.

Courage is essential for this journey. It calls us to confront the parts of ourselves we may fear to acknowledge or share. It takes us out of our comfort zones into a space of vulnerability and discomfort. Yet, in doing so, we open ourselves to profound transformation. We break down the barriers that hinder connections with others and our true selves. We pave the way for healing and growth, not just for ourselves but for those around us.

In high-pressure environments like the workplace, where toughness and silence about mental health struggles prevail, embracing openness and vulnerability becomes particularly powerful. Creating a culture that values these qualities fosters support for addressing mental health and emotional well-being. It leads to a compassionate and resilient workforce, better equipped to handle life's demands.

This transformation, however, is a challenging feat. It requires dedication to openness and vulnerability, a willingness to confront uncomfortable truths and embrace discomfort, and the building of empathy and understanding, as well as the recognition that our wounds are sources of strength and transformation.

So, let us embrace the power of openness, vulnerability, and transformation. Let us create a world that values empathy, compassion, and growth. And let us recognise that by opening up about our wounds, we hold the power to transform ourselves and our world. As we take up the torch of hope and healing, we become the missing piece in this stressful world, weaving together a collective work of good people ready to embrace the unspoken method of speaking and listening, fostering growth and well-being for all.

CHOICES AND CHANCES

"Would you tell me, please, which way I ought to go from here?' 'That depends a good deal on where you want to get to,' said the Cat. 'I don't much care where -' said Alice. 'Then it doesn't matter which way you go,' said the Cat. '- so long as I get SOMEWHERE,' Alice added as an explanation. 'Oh, you're sure to do that,' said the Cat, 'if you only walk long enough."
— **Lewis Carroll**, Alice in Wonderland

I was in my harness, which gripped loosely, but I still felt it hugging me. The African sunset was dropping below the Fingerboard on the derrick, making it around 3:00pm. You could smell the sweet aroma of steak and sticky chicken pouring along the gangway and up to the drill floor, pulsing from the galley into my nose, letting me know the day was almost done.

Bobby, the AD, walked towards me as the cement head moved up and down inside the rotary table. The compensator was running on auto to prevent the sea state from causing any damage to the drill string and down-hole tools, which were around forty thousand feet below us. The constant noise was calming and a present reminder that we were still working, even though it was relatively quiet on the drill floor. I was standing by the work basket, a large yellow telescopic machine designed to elevate two men off the deck and into the derrick to access the various tools we use for sending into the earth we'd drilled below the seabed. I still find it impressive how incredible this technology is. Still, having a gorgeous sunset warming your skin and giving a slight tan, a little lobster is even more special.

"Stevie McWeevy," Bobby said in his ultra-low voice, his smile as bright as the sun.

"Big lad, how's it going?" I replied. Bobby is six foot four and weighs around 20 stone of solid muscle. A big, wonderful African-American man whose laugh and humour always made my trips on the drill ship easier. He was one of the best lads on that crew, a fantastic AD, and he kept me learning when we worked hard.

"It's all good. Got my truck license and tractors ready for me back home in Mississippi, so it's only a matter of time!"

"So, you're going for it then."

"My man, it all comes down to simple things. We can all complain and bitch about how shit things are and how you're gonna get going. But if you're unhappy with your lot, take a goddamned chance. And if you don't like your chances, man, make a new choice!"

Although I was enjoying this quiet day, Bobby's words were startling.

"Bobby, I love that. Choices & Chances."

"That's it, man, 'cause nothing's gonna change unless you change it or yourself."

"I hear that." It made total sense to me.

I started to think about a few things I'd left unfinished: my memoir, my online courses, the live events I'd spoken at and didn't build on how I could have. My offshore career didn't pan out the way I had intended, but in truth, it was more about impressing my father, that I wanted to climb the ladder of success.

I remembered my idea about writing a book to help the offshore and energy industry understand mental health and well-being and all the talks and consulting I'd already done but hadn't ramped up or driven deeper to reach more clients. So much unfinished business. I shifted to personal stuff. I still needed to complete my garden, interior decorating, unhung pictures of me and my son, and all the piles of books and notes in my journals that filled up decades of thoughts and feelings, picking up dust. I even had a script for a Netflix series. It's one thing to be creative but needing more discipline to complete one thing made me consider my choices over the last few years.

Had I wasted all this time?

Was I living a life of procrastination? Why didn't I achieve the dreams and goals I had set out for myself? What was I going to do about it? These were the questions that plagued me. I reflected on the present moment and realised that my health was my biggest issue. Health is and always will be my most significant asset. Still, I was three stone overweight and using food as a coping mechanism for my internal stress and pressure, which was silently covering me. I knew my blood pressure wasn't tremendous, and I didn't want to stand on stage, fearing people would judge me for my big belly and fat cheeks.

Just then, Bobby, with his deep voice, captured my attention again, saying, "Yeah, Stevie McWeevy, I can see you thinking about all those things you wanna do but haven't done."

I asked Bobby, " What do you think it takes to make meaningful changes in life to achieve our desires?" I was curious to hear his thoughts.

Bobby smiled, gazing at the sun-drenched horizon while the gentle waves lapped at the boat's edge. "It takes courage, my friend. Courage to take a chance and make a choice. Even if things don't go according to plan, at least you dared to try."

His words resonated with me, and I felt a sense of vulnerability. I realised that I had known all along what I needed to do but lacked the courage to take that leap. Why? What was I waiting for? I knew I had it inside me to achieve more incredible things, but a tether around my mind prevented me from taking a leap into the light. I'd gained so much, but my drive to do more was stifled by my shortcomings, and I knew the fire was bubbling inside me again.

The truth was my career had hit a rough patch. Forty-two years old, I was still a roughneck offshore. But deep down, I knew I had untapped potential, and it was time to act.

It's easy to get caught up in our fears and doubts, to let our potential remain buried within us, becoming what I call "Graveyard Goblins: " the creative sparks we take to the grave. But we must have the courage to face our fears, make a choice, and take that first step towards our goals. Only then can we unlock our true potential and create a fulfilling life.

To make something of your life, you must take a chance or leave it to rot with the Graveyard Goblins. I realised I had been a spectator in my story for far too long, and it was time to get back into the game.

I shared my thoughts with Bobby, who agreed it was a simple outlook on life - choices and chances. Our conversation delved deeper into trusting our gut instincts, listening to opportunities, and having faith in something bigger than ourselves. Covered in dust and sweat from hard work, I was once again met with a working-class man who held wisdom from his life and was sharing it with me. Bobby reminded me that the big man upstairs sometimes works in the dark when we feel low and alone.

"But it takes time," he said, "and you're going to have to endure it to enjoy it."

As Bobby and I talked for hours, I soaked in his words of wisdom. We discussed the ups and downs of life and the importance of learning lessons from our failures. The wind shifted, and we leaned on the railings, enjoying the beautiful sunset. Suddenly, Bobby's demeanour turned as he gestured for us to prepare for the next task, reminding me that life is about balance between reflection and action. As the evening began to fall over us, I felt grateful for the opportunity to reflect on my choices and consider where I wanted to go.

Awakenings.

Later that night, I had a close call. I was looking for a hammer to change the saver subcomponent on the top drive. As the 60-ton piece of machinery descended to the rotary level on the drill floor, I turned around to search for the hammer, foolishly neglecting to look up. This was highly unusual for me as I always emphasised safety and the importance of being aware of one's surroundings. My old Toolpusher, Tony Santo, constantly drilled into me, "Look up and live."

The elevators, a large piece of equipment that clamps around the drill pipe, hit me squarely on the hard hat, causing me to react quickly and drop to the floor to avoid any serious injury. I hit the deck faster than Superman, racing to save Lois Lane from a bullet. I bounced back up, embarrassed and ashamed, knowing everyone had witnessed it.

The driller looked concerned, and I raised my hand, admitting it was my fault. Then Bobby said, "Not that kind of chance, Stevie Mcweevy." We both laughed, and he asked if I was okay. Although my ego and pride were wounded, the brush with death had a more profound impact.

The last two hours of my shift were spent in a strange space, my thoughts drifting to war, being shot at, making it home alive with all my limbs, and the numerous close calls with death that I had faced throughout my life. How many times did I need to feel close to death before I made the choice to take the chances that would improve the lives of those I care about and create the life and brand I have always dreamed of?

I enjoyed my job, but my body reminded me I was not immortal. The aches and pains of 30 years of labour were starting to take their toll. I needed a plan, a set of choices that would alter my chances.

It was a rare, weird day that leaves you feeling reflective. After my shift, I enjoyed a cigarette with the lads under the sun and ate a plate of steak and chips from the BBQ, which I barely touched. I made a cup of Earl Grey tea and took a shower. As I stood under the water, I noticed the bottle of shower gel, and there it was: "Awakenings" in bold letters on the back of the bottle. It felt like a message to stop wasting time and make significant changes and choices. It was time for me to bleed out the negativity in my life and share the message I had been carrying for years. It was time to open the bleed-off.

CONCLUSION

In the journey of opening the bleed-off, we have explored the transformative power of openness, vulnerability, and the wisdom held within our wounds. We have embraced the gentle courage needed to step into discomfort and confront our most profound truths. In doing so, we have discovered the deep healing and growth that comes from sharing our stories and connecting with others.

The unspoken method has been our guiding light on this path of self-discovery and collective evolution. It has shown us that true collaboration and connection are born from the depths of our vulnerability and honesty. In these spaces of openness, we find the missing piece of ourselves, woven together with the threads of compassion and understanding.

Collaboration is not just about working together; it is about listening to one another with empathy and compassion. When we allow ourselves to be vulnerable, we create an environment where others feel safe to do the same. In this safe space, we can collaborate, support each other, and find solutions that benefit all.

In today's fast-paced and often isolating world, the need for communication and genuine connection has never been greater. We are surrounded by noise and distractions, but at our core, we crave authentic human interaction. The unspoken method challenges us to cut through the noise to engage in meaningful conversations that heal and uplift.

As we lean into our wounds, we see that they hold the very wisdom we need to navigate life's challenges. They are not to be hidden or ignored but to be embraced and shared. In opening ourselves up, we find healing for our souls and become beacons of hope for others.

The unspoken method is not a quick fix or a one-size-fits-all solution. It is a journey of self-discovery, self-compassion, and growth. It requires patience, persistence, and a willingness to face discomfort. But it is a journey worth taking, for it leads us to a better version of ourselves—a more connected, compassionate, and resilient version.

So, let us continue to open the bleed-off, to speak of our experiences with gentle courage, and to lean into the wisdom held within our wounds. Let us embrace the power of collaboration and recognise that we find our strength in our vulnerability. Let us prioritise communication and genuine connection, knowing that it is through these heartfelt exchanges that we can make a real difference in the lives of others.

The unspoken method offers healing and the keys to unlocking a brighter, more compassionate world. It is an invitation to step into the fullness of our humanity, embrace our imperfections, and celebrate the beauty of our shared experiences.

Let us walk this path together, supporting and uplifting one another. In our collective journey, we find the true power of openness—the power to heal, grow, and create a more connected and compassionate world for all.

STANDING TALL

A Tribute to the Heroes of the Oil and Gas Industry

My dear friends, I will speak to you now as this is from the heart. I will keep my words simple and clear.

Amidst the roaring waves of the energy sector, there stand men and women whose unwavering commitment fuels the world's progress. You are the unsung heroes of our modern era, the backbone of an industry that powers nations and drives economies forward. You are the brave souls of the oil and gas industry.

For far too long, your sacrifices have gone unnoticed; your struggles brushed aside amidst the relentless pursuit of profit and progress. But today, in the pages of "Open the Bleed Off," we honour your unwavering devotion, relentless spirit, and unyielding resilience.

To the men and women who toil tirelessly on offshore rigs, your hands weathered by the relentless sea breeze, your backs bent under the weight of heavy machinery, we salute you. You brave the elements daily, risking life and limb to extract the black gold that powers our world.

The hours spent under crashing waves and nights so long and cold you can feel your soul aching for the warmth of home. Delays and deadlines are so fierce you wonder why you ever climbed on board that rusty rig. To the heat of summer when you pull out of the hole wet, covered in baking hot mud, wrapped in a blue suit, making you a walking, talking sauna and still expected to push through for another 7 hours. From the times you almost lost a finger to the days you watched a mate being sent home in the chopper as he was nearly killed. To the days you heard of a mate who never made it. I stand with you, quietly respectful of your drive and passion.

To those who labour in the scorching heat of desert fields, your faces smeared with sweat and dust, your eyes squinting against the blinding sun, we applaud you. You endure the harsh conditions of the arid landscape, drilling deep into the earth's crust to unearth the precious resources that fuel our industries.

To the brave souls who venture into the depths of the earth, descending into dark and narrow tunnels, your hands steady as you navigate the labyrinth of underground passages, we honour you. You delve into the unknown, extracting the lifeblood of our civilization from the depths of the earth's core.

To the men and women onboard the vessels and brave those demanding seas and oceans to supply and navigate the energy where it needs to be, you are the life source of our work. Without you, we couldn't be. To the teams who serve us the banquets and beds we call home for half our lives, you are the family who keeps us alive and fed and, at times, laugh as we complain about a lack of eggs, steak, and coco pops.

To the pilots, who carry us like little birdies to our cages in the sea. How brave you are to watch over our souls sometimes during the summer when the oceans look like a blanket of glass, calm and serene. Others, in the dead of night under the storms and rain where you can't even see past the following prayer. Yet you navigate us back to our families. Thank you.

But amidst the industry's triumphs, a shadow is cast by the ever-present spectre of stress and uncertainty. As wages dwindle and hours stretch longer, as roles become twinned and demands multiply, the men and women of the oil and gas industry find themselves caught in a relentless tide of pressure and strain.

Yet, despite your challenges, you stand tall, spirits unbroken, your resolve unwavering. They are the true embodiment of resilience, the living testament to the indomitable human spirit.

In "Open the Bleed Off," we pay homage to these unsung heroes, offering insights and strategies to help them navigate the turbulent waters of their profession. We acknowledge your sacrifices, struggles, and triumphs and offer them the support and guidance they need to thrive in an industry that demands nothing less than your best.

To the men and women of the oil and gas industry, I say this: You are not alone. Your struggles are my struggles, and your victories are our victories. Together, we will stand tall against the tide, united in our pursuit of a brighter, more resilient future.

So, let us raise our voices in tribute to these brave souls, honour your sacrifices, and stand together in solidarity as we embark on a journey of hope, healing, and transformation.

You are the true oil and gas industry heroes, and your legacy will endure for generations.

Thank you for embarking on this transformative journey through the unspoken method with me. As we've explored the power of openness, vulnerability, and healing, I believe we have touched upon a profound truth—one that has the potential to create a seismic shift within your workplace.

Imagine bringing the unspoken method directly to your team. Picture the impact of fostering a culture where authenticity and compassion are celebrated and embraced as cornerstones of success. I've witnessed this transformation first hand by sharing the unspoken method with other organisations.

Hundreds of people from diverse backgrounds and industries have decided to speak more openly and with deeper care. They found that by embracing openness and genuine communication, they created an environment where collaboration flourished, mental health was nurtured, and their teams achieved new heights of productivity.

The unspoken method is not just a passing trend—it's a movement shaping the future of workplaces. Now is the time to open the bleed-off and let the healing begin. Inviting me to your workplace can unlock the potential for growth, connection, and transformation.

During our time together, I will share real-life stories, practical strategies, and actionable steps that will empower each member of your team to tap into the wisdom within their own wounds. Together, we'll learn how to create safe spaces for open dialogues, nurture empathy, and build a resilient and supportive workforce.

The unspoken method isn't about sweeping problems under the rug or pretending everything is perfect. It's about facing challenges with courage and vulnerability and finding strength in our shared experiences. By doing so, we unleash the collective power of our humanity and create a workplace that values the well-being and growth of every individual.

So, let's take the next step together. Please reach out and open the bleed-off within your organisation. Let's create a workplace where every voice is heard, every struggle is acknowledged, and every person is empowered to thrive.

The unspoken method can unlock a new level of authenticity, connection, and fulfilment within your team. I can't wait to be a part of this transformative journey with you.

BONUS CHAPTER

THE BEAUTY OF PAIN: UNVEILING THE MOST FUNDAMENTAL REALITY

"What's the most real of what matters? How about pain? Why is it the most real? Try arguing it away — good luck. So, pain is the fundamental reality. Alright, well, that's rough. But doesn't it lead to nihilism and hopelessness? Yeah, doesn't it lead to a philosophy that's antithetical towards being? The most fundamental reality is pain. Yes, is there anything more fundamental than pain? Love. Really, love and truth. That's what you've got. And you know, if they're more powerful than pain, maybe they're the most real things." - Jordan Peterson.

Hearing Jordan Peterson speaking on pain, I was truly inspired to learn he holds the feelings of love and truth above them. It's hard to live with pain. You will have been around much of it, no doubt, not just in work or life but mostly in your personal life. Loss, change, and setbacks come with pain sewn into their experience. But this is not enough for you to quit being kind to yourself. Pain is a reflective presence as it mirrors the moments that hold value to your existence. You care about the people in your life and want to do well. When pain enters your present, it takes away the capacity to think correctly about who you are. This can make it a fearful encounter; fear mixed with pain is a recipe for suffering.

In human experience, certain truths transcend the barriers of philosophy, culture, and time. One such reality, eloquently articulated by Jordan Peterson, asserts that pain is a cornerstone of existence. It's the most real of what matters. But why is pain granted such a profound status, and how does its prominence shape our perspective on life? Let's embark on a journey through these contemplations, for within them lies the essence of resilience, growth, and the very fabric of our humanity.

Imagine attempting to argue away pain's existence. Peterson's challenge echoes in our minds, daring us to question its inevitability. We hit an impasse in our endeavour to rationalise it out of existence. Pain is a relentless, undeniable force. It can't be neatly brushed aside or deconstructed through mere intellectual discourse. It exists, and its existence holds power.

Yet, as Peterson acknowledges, acknowledging pain's centrality raises disquieting questions. Does it lead to nihilism, a bleak worldview that renders existence meaningless? Indeed, contemplating pain's pre-eminence can evoke a sense of hopelessness, a seemingly grim outlook on life's purpose. But what if pain is a gateway to understanding deeper truths?

Within pain's shadow, other profound concepts emerge—love and truth. These, Peterson suggests, possess the potential to rival pain's supremacy. Consider the monumental experiences of love and truth. They resonate as intensely real, perhaps even more so than pain itself. Love's power to heal and uplift truth's ability to pierce through illusion both hold the potential to transcend and transform the human experience.

This juxtaposition might make us wonder: Are love and truth more powerful than pain? Could they be the bedrock of existence if they can eclipse pain's dominion? Could they be the most authentic aspects of life?

In weaving these thoughts, Peterson offers a revelation. Pain, as natural and formidable as it is, cannot stand alone as the pinnacle of existence. Love and truth, with their potent capacities, emerge as contenders for this throne. If they can overpower pain and shine brighter in the face of darkness, they are the true constants, the enduring truths that shape our lives.

Pain becomes a canvas upon which the brushstrokes of love and truth can shine more brightly. It becomes a teacher, a catalyst for growth, a messenger that propels us toward greater understanding and compassion. The human experience, with all its intricacies, gains depth and meaning when pain is no longer an isolated reality but a part of a larger narrative.

This chapter delves into the beauty of pain, not to glorify suffering or trivialise its impact but to unveil its role as an integral thread in the tapestry of existence. We explore the interplay between pain, love, and truth, contemplating how these concepts intersect and inform our perception of reality. Through the lens of Peterson's insight, we embrace the complexity of human experience, acknowledging that pain is neither an adversary nor an ultimate reality but a transformative force that can guide us toward the profound truths that matter.

FINAL THOUGHTS

Embracing the Wisdom of Our Wounds

As you journey through life, you come face to face with your wounds, your imperfections, and your pain. It is easy to perceive these aspects of yourself as enemies, as signs of weakness that you must hide from the world. But as you pause and reflect, you realise these wounds are not the adversaries you once believed them to be. Instead, they hold within them the most profound gift—wisdom.

Your wounds are not a mark of failure or inadequacy; they are the imprints of your experiences and the stories of your resilience. In each scar lies a tale of survival, a lesson learned, and an opportunity to grow. Your pain is not a burden to be discarded; it is a wellspring of compassion and understanding that connects you to the shared human experience.

When you recognise your wounds, you embark on self-discovery and self-acceptance. You acknowledge that perfection is an illusion and that your struggles are the raw material for transformation. In facing your vulnerabilities, you discover your true strength, for it takes courage to confront the darkest corners of your soul.

Embracing your wounds is an act of radical authenticity. It is an invitation to be honest, flawed, and beautifully imperfect. Your scars are not meant to be hidden in shame; they are the emblems of your authenticity, testaments to the battles you have fought and continue to wage. Some you win and others you lose. Always you grow.

In these wounds, you find the well of empathy from which compassion flows abundantly. The wisdom gleaned from your pain allows us to reach out to others with genuine understanding and support. Your experiences become bridges, connecting you to others who walk similar paths, creating a web of shared humanity.

When you dare to embrace your wounds, you unleash the infinite resources of resilience, love, and hope that lies dormant within. It is like striking a hidden reservoir deep within the earth—the energy of transformation gushes forth, nourishing your soul and watering the seeds of change in the world around you.

The wisdom of your wounds is not meant to be hoarded; it is a gift meant to be shared. As you tap into this wellspring of insight, compassion, and strength, you become a vessel through which healing and positive change flow into the world. Your stories inspire others to embark on self-discovery, self-acceptance, and growth journeys.

The journey of embracing your wounds is not without its challenges. It requires you to confront the shadows within, face your pain with vulnerability, and shed the armour that once protected you. But in doing so, you liberate yourself from the shackles of fear and shame, stepping into the light of authenticity and empowerment.

As you close this book, I invite you to embrace your wounds with an open heart. Allow the wisdom they carry to flow through you, enriching your life and the lives of those around you. Embrace your imperfections, for they are the brushstrokes that paint the masterpiece of your life. See your pain not as an enemy but as a teacher—an invaluable guide on your growth journey.

In Don's last few months, we can only imagine the words and thoughts he must have felt and held deep. He had always been the pillar of strength and support for others, but now, he seemed burdened by an inner struggle he couldn't share. Despite the media and social chattering of a world that pretends to be open, Don never asked for help. Instead, he carried his pain in silence until it became unbearable, leading him to make a devastating decision that left his family and friends shattered.

The weight of Don's absence now rests heavily upon his family, and the wounds left behind are deep and profound. His loved one's grapple with the haunting question of whether they could have done more to reach out to him, to understand the turmoil he was facing. Caitlin, his daughter, bravely shares her own journey of grief and loss, reflecting on her father's life and untimely passing. In a poignant conversation with me on the Wounded podcast, Caitlin emphasised the critical need for open discussions about mental health and the importance of speaking up when we struggle.

Don's story is a powerful reminder that even the strongest among us can be silently battling their demons. It is a heartbreaking example of how society's expectations of stoicism and strength can lead individuals to conceal their pain, fearing judgment or appearing weak. Don's decision not to ask for help serves as a poignant lesson about the importance of breaking free from the shackles of societal norms and encouraging open dialogue about mental health. I am reminded of my own shortcomings back when I left the army after serving in war twice and holding tightly to my pain from fear of seeming weak to those I cared about. Unable to fix myself or unleash the burdens of my life, I am given this chance to share what frightens me most now. The wounds I carry today are the documentation of my need to find a way to bring us closer together and share the wisdom I have learned from myself, in life, and mostly from others.

Caitlin's journey through grief and healing reflects the profound impact her father's loss has had on her life. It highlights the urgency of addressing mental health issues openly and compassionately, not just for those currently struggling but also for the loved ones left behind after a tragic loss.

In the wake of Don's passing, Caitlin finds solace in sharing her story, spreading awareness about mental health, and advocating for open conversations. The wounded podcast became a platform for her to express her pain, vulnerability, and commitment to preventing others from experiencing the same heartbreak.

Listening to Caitlin's powerful narrative reminds us that mental health is not an isolated concern but a shared responsibility. Each of us can play a role in breaking down the barriers that prevent people from seeking help. It starts with fostering a culture of empathy and understanding, where vulnerability is not seen as a weakness but as a courageous act of self-preservation.

Don's story and Caitlin's courage open our eyes to the profound impact of our actions and inactions. We must learn to read between the lines, recognising the subtle signs that someone we care about may be silently struggling. Let us be present and ready to extend a helping hand, a listening ear, or a compassionate heart to those who most need it.

The embers of empathy burn within each of us, waiting to be stoked into flames of change. By coming together, sharing our stories, and speaking openly about mental health, we can create a world where no one feels alone or afraid to ask for help. Let us honour Don's memory by breaking the silence and creating a space where healing can flourish, and hope can thrive.

May the wisdom of your wounds be the catalyst for positive change in your life and the world. May you find the courage to be vulnerable, the strength to heal, and the compassion to connect deeply with others. May you always remember that your wounds are not a sign of weakness but a testament to the incredible strength that lives within you.

As you step forth each day as you walk or drive to work, as you take the bus or cycle to your job and into the day, carrying the wisdom of your wounds in your heart, may you be a beacon of hope, love, and transformation for all who seek to make a change. This change starts from within and ripples out, touching the lives of countless souls.

Opening the bleed-off is not the end of your story but the beginning of change. It is simply the idea that a single person can help another. And in this world, under these circumstances, that is all that matters. Like any significant movement or change, the transformation begins with you.

Printed in Great Britain
by Amazon